Tails of a Cow Doc

John E. Crawley, DVM

Tails of a Cow Doc

John E. Crawley, DVM

Edited by Olive Crawley and Kevin Crawley
Foreword by Kevin Crawley
Afterword by Katie Crawley
Tails of Another Cow Doc by Gerald Crawley

Clan Crawley Publishing
2015

First Printing: 2015

ISBN 978-1-312-95584-4

Clan Crawley Publishing
2040 N. Dubuque Road
Iowa City, IA 52245

www.dawoods.com/cowdoc

Contents

Foreword

I had asked Mom to write this foreword, but when I was putting everything together, I thought what she wrote was better on the back cover than anything I had been able to come up with. So, she gets the outside, and that leaves me room to make some production notes. We've tried to keep the editing to a minimum, mostly fixing typos and punctuation, and shortening a run-on sentence or two. Arrangement of the stories was based on the filenames (the last story is from the file 'cowdoc36').

When I was transferring the files from his computer, I found a letter that Dad's brother Jerry had written to friends. I don't know if Dad put it there on purpose, but it does add more perspective on Dad and his stories, and we feel it is a fitting tribute to a brother with whom he shared so much, and who passed away just five months later.

As we do see this as a tribute as well as a memoir, we've also included the obituary that my sister Katie wrote for Dad's funeral. She covers a lot about Dad that his stories leave out.

Katie also took the photo of Dad with the cowboy hat and pipe when she was still in college, and it's one that we've all felt most captured Doc. Doug Schell took the photo of Mom and Dad on the back cover, and Mom took the photo of the license plate with her trusty iPod.

Here you go: the culmination of ten years of writing on Dad's part, five years of follow-up on Mom's part, and several years of editing by multiple family members. We hope you enjoy it.

Kevin Crawley
April, 2015

Section One: Vet School

Chapter 1

I have been fortunate in the fact that I knew from high school that I wanted to be a veterinarian. I knew where I wanted to go, but how to get a there was the problem. When I started to apply at Iowa State in 1948, they required only one year of pre-vet study. I attended Whitewater State Teachers College and took the mandatory requirements. I had letters of recommendation from the county agent, my high school and a veterinarian. Unfortunately, they had changed the entrance requirements, and I was not qualified.

I transferred to the University of Wisconsin and enrolled. Someone blew it, and I was in the pre-med program rather than pre-vet. Wisconsin did not have a veterinary school so I was forced to apply to the out-of-state schools. I got the entrance requirements for University of Minnesota, Iowa State, Michigan State and the University of Illinois, and for the next two years, I took courses that would satisfy those requirements.

During the first semester of my junior year, I was working for Dr. Banner Bill Morgan in his parasitology lab, cleaning glassware from fecal exams. One day he asked me what my major was, and when I told him pre-vet, he informed me that I would never get into vet school unless I was enrolled in the College of Agriculture, rather than the College of Letters and Science. So I transferred, and he was my adviser. He said that if I took his Vet Science 30 (parasitology) and did well, he would make sure I got into a veterinary school and graduate from ag school with a Bachelor of Science degree. I thought that my prayers were answered and all my problems solved, but fate would not have it, and it was not to be. I got a 98 on his final exam, but Dr. Morgan died suddenly from viral pneumonia while on a train trip to the west coast during the summer. When I returned to school in the fall of 1950, my new adviser was Dr. Erskin Morris, a bacteriologist who knew nothing of Dr. Morgan's plans for me and

John E. Crawley, DVM

wasn't at all interested in helping me.

Here I was, in my senior year in college, without a major and with a great number of credits in various courses. I studied the major requirements, and found the closest one I could meet was an Animal Science major. However, there were requirements to graduate with a degree from the College of Agriculture that I had to meet, plus the additional courses that I could not take because I had not taken the prerequisite courses.

I went to the Dean of the College of Agriculture and told Dean Kevlin my sad story. I had to take 18 credits to have the enrollment requirements waived, or substitute other courses for major requirements. He is said he would take care of all the problems, and he did. At the start of the second semester, I call on him again to make changes and allow 19 credits, and again he took care of all of it. I was a second-semester senior and I was taking some freshmen courses to fulfill the ag school requirements. One course was Biochemistry 5, which was a substitute for Home Economics. I could not attend the laboratory portions of the course, because I had another subject during those hours, so I would go into the lab when no one else was around at night and do the experiments required.

I sent applications to Iowa State, the University of Minnesota and the University of Illinois. I had taken a French course because it was required by the University of Illinois, and it was one of the hardest courses I ever taken, because it was also required by pre-med students. I got a postcard back from Illinois, stating they did not accept out-of-state students in the school of veterinary medicine, but I did receive conditional acceptance from Iowa State and the University of Minnesota. I had not seen nor heard from Dr. Morris since that first day, but now I received a call that I should come to his office. He had been informed of my acceptance at both schools, and he told me unless I accepted at one or the other in the next few days, he would write them and I would not be accepted in either. I pondered for two days over the pros and cons of each, and finally decided to go to Iowa State College. I paid Dean Kevlin one more visit and ask that

I be allowed to graduate cum laude. I had the grades and all the credits, but I had only enrolled in the College of Agriculture for three semesters instead of four. He smiled and said, "You will know, and I will know you graduated cum laude, but it will never be on your diploma."

Chapter 2

Four days later, I had shaken the dust of the University of Wisconsin and Madison from my shoes; I was on my way to Ames Iowa. I was traveling by train on the Soo Line, carrying my trombone, suitcase and steamer trunk. I had to hire the only taxi in town to get my stuff to the campus. I got settled in the men's dormitory, Fraley Hall which held over 1200 young men and alas, no girls.

Two days later I reported to the Vet Quadrangle. There were four wings and a huge open square in the center, with the statue of the Gentle Doctor. The Anatomy Wing was located on the left side, and consisted of a large concrete amphitheater, which was the lecture hall for Gross Anatomy. Adjacent to it was a large open room, where I would spend many hours in the next nine months. This was theAnatomy Laboratory; the home of dissected dogs, horses, cows and pigs. In the lecture hall, the stone benches had little pads to sit upon, and were extremely uncomfortable. God help you if you ever went to sleep. Dr. Robert Getty, our professor, would be standing down in front of us and he was extremely accurate with his right hand. He could hit a student who was eight rows up right in the chest with a chunk of meat. He was a tall, handsome man with a little mustache in his late 40's and always well dressed. However, he had a nasty streak. One day he called upon a student named Sprugel, who had not read the assignment for the day. The student admitted it, and Dr. Getty kept asking questions, and each time the student admitted he had not read the chapter. Sprugel dropped out of school soon after, but for months, Dr. Getty would call "Mr.Sprugel". When no one answered, he would grin and say, "That's right, he's not here anymore."

The second portion of the wing contained a conventional lecture room, and a room filled with desks and microscopes. This was the bailiwick of Dr. Faust and his handmaid, Rose. He was of small stature, slightly overweight, and in his 70's. We all thought of him as

4

being an eight foot-tall giant. He taught us Microscopic Anatomy and the room was filled with slides. Rose walked with a limp, and the students said she had gotten that way by stamping on slides so they were unintelligible. One day while lecturing to us about the microscopic anatomy of a horse's hoof for about 20 minutes he cried, "Rose you have the slide on upside-down", and started all over again. He retired after all our sophomore year and we never saw him again.

The School of veterinary medicine operated on the honor system, so the professors would merely write the questions on the chalkboard and leave. Tests were never announced, but when you went to class and saw the dreaded blue books on the table, you knew you were in for a bad day. The exams lasted three to four hours, and they took great delight in springing them on us at the most inopportune times. They gave us one the day were to leave for home at Thanksgiving. We finished up about 5:00, and drove back to Wisconsin. Another big surprise was the day after we returned from Christmas; it was on the anatomy of the central system of the dog. They had one other favorite, which was known as a "tag quiz", where they would put tags on various parts of dissected animals. You were given 20 seconds to identify each one, and then move on to the next cadavers. There would be about 75 tags to identify, and if you fail to specify right or left, it was counted as wrong.

The last club they held over our heads was the oral exam given at the end of each quarter. You entered the professor's office in pairs and they would ask a question of each of you. I remember the first one they asked me. Dr. Getty remarked, "It's sure cold out there today." When I agreed, he asked, "How can you tell? Tell me the musculature and innervation of the senses involved."

Classes started at 7:30 each morning, and finished at 4:30 in the afternoon, five days a week. On Saturdays, we had just a half a day. However, each night, the Gross Anatomy Laboratory would be filled with students doing their dissections, sometimes even on Saturdays and Sundays. We usually spent at least three hours every night with the books. Since they could give you an exam anytime they felt like it, you had to be prepared. There was one big exception; we were all

5

John E. Crawley, DVM

expected to attend the junior AVMA (American Veterinary Medical Association) meetings, which were held once a month. It was an unwritten law there could be no exams on the day after the meeting, so the vet students would head in mass to downtown Ames, and Stover's lounge. They served 3.2 beer, but if you drank enough, the end result was the same.

There was one other class - Veterinary ROTC (Reserve Officers Training Corps). It was required of all freshmen and sophomores unless you had previous military service. If you enrolled in your junior and senior years, you were obligated to serve at least two years on active duty. You were paid at the rate of 90 cents a day for the last two years. You were also required to attend six weeks of summer camp sometime between your freshman and senior years. I was very aware that after one year of school, I was limited as to where I could work, so why not go to camp right away? This meant that upon graduation, I would have to spend two years in the military. I went to visit the head of the local draft board, a farmer by the name of Frank Kipp who told me, "Don't do it. We need a new veterinarian in the county, as the others are getting old."

It's a good thing I did not heed his advice, because after graduation, the draft board felt I was ripe for picking. I had been commissioned as a First Lieutenant in the Air Force Reserve, and was to report for active duty in August, but they would not believe me until I could show them my commission, signed by the president. I served my two years, which is a later story, and was home for year before the commission arrived.

In June after my freshman year, I reported to Fort Sam Houston in San Antonio TX along with two of my classmates from Iowa State, a farm boy, John Conley and a city boy, George Baron. I had one delightful experience in Texas. The first week, three of us were sent to the Gebhardt Packing Company, to observe the slaughter of cattle and goats. It was a small-enough plant that we could watch the entire process, from slaughtering to hanging the carcasses in the cooler. George had just purchased a new Argus C3 camera and was busily taking pictures of the large Hispanics who were working there, and they eagerly posed for him. After a short while one of them cut off a piece of small intestine and threw it in a small sink with steam bubbling through the water. It was a place where they were sterilized their knives after cutting through an abscess, and didn't look very appetizing to us. The young USDA veterinarian told us they considered this to be a great delicacy, and they would be very offended if we didn't eat it. We explained that they had not cleaned out the intestine before putting it into the boiling water, but he said they believed that the foods did not go through this portion of the intestine. Unfortunately, they could not explain how it got from the stomach to the rectum without passing through the intestines. As soon as it was cooked and floated on top of the scummy water, they brought it over to us on a piece of paper towel and cut into small pieces. I suggested that it should be sterile after being boiled and I would try it if the other two fellows would. Being a farm boy, Johnny had no reservations, but George was a bit more reluctant. We got a saltcellar and after liberal use, we ate it all. When we got back to camp that night, we advised the rest of our classmates not to take pictures at the Gebhardt Plant. Now, tested but unbowed, if anyone says something tastes like shit, I can tell them, "I have eaten shit, and it tastes better than this."

Chapter 3

As I returned for the sophomore year, there was a bit of dreaded anticipation. What next? Ward, Al and I had decided to room together in Frealy Hall. Our classes all moved across the courtyard to the other side of the Quadrangle, where we met to an entirely new group of professors. There was Dr. Packer and his assistant, Doctor Collier, who would be our instructors in Bacteriology. Dr. Benbrook would teach us Pathology and Parasitology, and Dr. Hewlett, with his assistant, Dr. Lloyal Cob Payne, would handle Physiology. In the spring quarter, we would have Dr. Frank Ramsey for Special Pathology, and L. Meyer Jones for Pharmacology. We had not met in any of these doctors before, and had no idea what to expect from any of them.

Doctors Packer and Collier were fair but demanding, but Dr. Benbrook was a whole different matter. He was very sarcastic and demeaning to all of us. He had flunked his own son from Iowa State, so that he had to go to Kansas State to graduate. (I met him years later, as he had become a Veterinary Pathologist with the U.S. government.) I also believe he had flunked my old mentor, Dr. Banner Bill Morgan, who never did become a veterinarian, but received a PhD in Parasitology. One of my classmates received a "D" in Pathology, and when he went to question the grade, he was told that he had fallen asleep in class. The student denied it vehemently, and Dr. Benbrook stated, "You have a cough that irritates me." The grade was never changed. When writing an exam in his class, if a word was misspelled, the entire question was marked wrong. Needless to say, I had very little respect for him as a man and I avoided him as much as possible.

Dr. Hewlett was a very quiet, little old man, who spoke very slowly and softly. Dr. Payne was a breath of fresh air, and the Crown Prince of practical jokes. I can only imagine what the rest of the stogie old professors thought of him. He had run track at Kansas State and had the looks of a runner. He told everyone he was part Apache Indian and used a sun lamp to enhance his appearance. He had received an undergraduate degree in psychology and used to love to play with our minds. He gave one quiz of 50 true or false questions, with 49 being true. Another time, we were to define parts and functions of the heart in three words or less. The tests were never returned and if you wanted to see them you had to go to his office. I went to check one and I must the been the only one, because when we received the final exam, it was exactly the same with one additional question. I received a hundred percent and an "A" in a six-credit course. He can be also taught a course for graduate students in Zoology, and he would tell us how he would BS them, so you would question some of the things he told us. Every spring, there was a college-wide celebration called VEISHA, and all the departments set up displays. In our freshman year, we had worked hours and hours on a display of the nervous system of the dog. Dr. Payne brought several cages of chickens and labeled them with fictitious names, such as "the champion fighting cock of Story County," or a "rare naked neck African Zilby". He had a beaker of mercury that had he poured blood on, and when he placed a weight on it, it floated. He labeled it "elephant's blood" to explain why elephants weighed so much. Dr. Jones never left an impression on me one way or the other, but I always felt the professors were shoveling out knowledge with a scoop shovel and I was trying to pick up with a teaspoon.

My class schedule in the second year allowed us one afternoon a week and Saturdays off. My roommates and I decided to get jobs. I was saving for an engagement ring that I knew my parents would never give me a penny for, and after four years it was time to decorate her finger. The best-paying jobs on campus were at the physical plant, where the foreman favored hiring vet students. He felt we were older and more dependable. We received $1.15 an hour, and we more than earned it. We dug ditches, built stone walls, tore up concrete with a jackhammer and unloaded coal cars with scoop shovels. I'll never forget one Saturday morning, when my roommates had been "over-served" the previous night and were suffering the after-effects. We were using a jackhammer to dig a ditch and they were suffering so much we almost gave up drinking. Usually, every evening after dinner we would take a nap, go down to the grill in the dorm and drink coffee, and then go back to our room and study till 1:00 when the rooms were quiet.

I had met Olive when she was a student nurse at St. Mary's Hospital on a blind date. We had dated for two years in Madison before I left for Ames. After her graduation, she returned home to Reedsburg to work in the local hospital and live with her mother and sisters. The last two years, ours had been a long-distance romance. I wrote a letter to her sister to ask her ring size, and had my roommate address the envelope so she would not know it was from me. I had written to ask what she would like for Christmas, and her answer was a nice pearl ring. I was sure she had read the letter to her sister and I thought, "if you want a pearl ring that is what you will get." I went to the five and dime store and bought a cheap and gaudy one, and put it in the case that the diamond came in. All the fellows in the dorm thought it was a great joke. I went to visit her the night I got home, and in the car I asked if she wanted her Christmas present, and when she said yes I gave it to her. I had the diamond ring in my pocket and as I wasn't sure what would happen next. Fortunately, it was rather dark and she couldn't see it clearly, but she graciously thanked me and said it was lovely and just what she wanted. I kissed her and gave her the diamond ring. She kept the fake pearl ring for a long time, and she swore she had not seen my letter and that she really wanted a pearl ring. To this day, she never has gotten one; perhaps sometimes soon. We were married on the fifth day of September, had a two day honeymoon and went back to work T.B. testing cows until we left for Ames.

We moved into University Housing in Pammel Court in old Army buildings. Ours was 451, and right next to the Union Pacific Railroad line. It ran less than 25 ft. from our bedroom but fortunately it was above us, and we were so tired, we never heard the trains at night. During the day, all conversation would cease until they went by, but everyone accepted this as a matter of course. All of the buildings were filled with married college students and a large number of them had children, so it got the nickname "Pablum Court". All of us were poor as church mice, and our entertainment was to visit the neighbors on Saturday night and watch George Gobel. Olive worked as a nurse in the College Hospital and we got along fine because we were young and in love.

Chapter 4

I finished my second year at Vet school, and was a master of bacteriology, parasitology, physiology, pharmacology, biochemistry and poisonous plants. But I had no experience in the realms of very practical veterinary medicine. I was not looking forward to another summer of shoveling gravel into cement mixers, so I decided to apply for a position with the State Department of Agriculture as a TB tester.

Every cow in Wisconsin is tested for tuberculosis once every five years. The tests are conducted on a countywide basis and are usually done by practicing veterinarians. However, in some counties the testing is not done, so the state hires people to conduct the tests in the summer. The test is done by injecting a small drop of tuberculin into the skin beneath the tail, and 72 hours later you examine the injection site for any reaction. If there is any swelling, it is evidence of tuberculosis and the animal must be destroyed.

I was sent to spend a week with Dr. Kennely, a state veterinarian, to learn how to administer the test. Things were going famously until the third day, when Dr. Holmes, a federal veterinarian, joined us to examine some cows that he had tested previously. The first herd we visited were purebred Jersey cattle that had been tested for John's Disease, and as Dr. Holmes examined each cow he told me to brand them. I was to place a large "J" on the side of their face, which meant they were to be destroyed.

Mr. Hasslinger, the owner kept asking, "What are you doing?" Dr. Holmes refused to answer. Needless to say, the owner became more upset with each passing minute, and I was beginning to fear for our lives. The farmer was a huge man, standing nearly 6 feet 4. His eyes were blazing, and the veins on his face and neck were pulsating. We left in a hurry and I've never found out what the outcome was.

The next stop was at a family farm with the parents, two grown sons, and their families milking a herd of purebred Holstein cattle. These animals had been injected for tuberculosis, and again Dr. Holmes examined them and told me to brand them. We condemned over 40 head. The state was to pay them a indemnity of hundred dollars a head. Unfortunately, the state did not have enough funds at that time.

I was sent to the house to pickup the purebred papers, and the grandmother graciously offered me a glass of milk. I politely refused, knowing that the entire herd had tuberculosis. I suggested to Dr. Holmes that the people be told of the danger to their health, but he said it was none of our business. I immediately lost any respect I had for him. Later that summer, I learned that the grandmother and two grandchildren were hospitalized with tuberculosis.

Chapter 5

I reported to the State Veterinarian's office in the Capitol building in Madison and met Dr. Harry O'Connell; a small wiry Irishman in his sixties, who gave me my working orders and equipment. I was issued two pair of coveralls, a pair of rubber boots, a tuberculin syringe, a tagging pliers, 1000 ear tags, lariat, plastic pail and boot brush, along with a large number of forms to be filled out.

I was surprised to see another student who was in school in the class ahead of me, and was going to work for the state also. We were to report to doctor Zeibell in Tomah, who would be our supervisor for the summer, as he was the State Veterinarian for this area. Jack would work in Monroe County while I was to go to Jackson County.

The county seat was Black River Falls, so I found a room there. We were to test 1000 head a week, which meant injecting 300 head for three days and checking them three days later. Jackson County was not noted for its dairy population; there were probably hundred deer for every cow. There was only one veterinarian for the entire county and he had not tested a cow. They were all mine to test.

I purchased a plat book and started to line up herds to check the next day. To test three hundred head, I needed about 15 farms. The farmers did not want to keep the cattle in the barn and any longer than necessary, so you had to have an early start. The first place I went was Paul Schliesner, who had about twenty-five head of Holsteins. I then proceeded to all the farms in the neighborhood, the one next door was owned by Oswald Snick, who was a very friendly fellow.

Three days later, when I read the test there were three animals at Paul's that showed swelling in the infected cow's injection site. I had never seen nor felt a positive reaction but I was very suspicious. We were told to notify doctor Zeibell if there were any questions, as we were not allowed to condemn, so I notified him.

When I went over to Snick's he asked me if I had found anything that morning and where I had been? I thought this a little strange and as I went to the neighboring farmers they also were curious. I came to find out most of them had been to Paul's and had checked the cows!

That afternoon Dr. Zeibell, as well as Dr. Schmovitz, the local vet, and a recently graduated vet were all waiting for me in Paul's barn. Each one checked all the cows while I waited and wondered. Had I made a colossal mistake or had I done a great job? Dr. Zeibell smiled and congratulated me.

Chapter 6

I tested over 11,000 head of cattle that summer and found only one other reactor, but I had an ingenious farmer who tried to convince me otherwise. He had an old cow that he was going to ship to the stockyards and decided it would be nice to get an extra $50 for her from the state. So he took some hornets in a bottle and stung her under the tail. However when I examined her, the swelling was entirely different. I smiled at him and said, "Nice try."

After Paul had shipped the three reactors, and before he could get paid by the state, he had to clean and disinfect the barn with a lye solution. I had to inspect it and fill out more papers. We discussed at length how the cattle could have become infected and reached no conclusion. I noticed there were several Bantam chickens in the barn. They roosted on the stanchions, with their droppings going into the mangers. I inquired how old the birds were and he told me they had been around for years. I knew that old chickens were subject to avian tuberculosis and could sensitize cattle to the tubercular test. I suggested that he bring me a couple of the birds and I would examine them, so one afternoon he showed up with a gunnysack and three dead Bantams. I had never seen the lesions of tuberculosis in chickens, but I had dressed enough birds in my youth to know what a healthy bird looked like. I posted them with my jackknife and found suspicious spots on the liver, which I suspected to be tuberculosis. I took the birds to Dr. Schmovitz, who confirmed my suspicions. He asked me where they came from. When I told him Paul's he shook his head and said. "Nice job".

I quickly found out when dealing with farmers, it paid to have a sense of humor, especially when the joke's on you. One day, we were down in in a pasture with a small creek running through it, chasing some young stock to the barn. When I attempted to jump the stream, I fell full length in the mud. When I looked up the farmer was doing his best to stop laughing. I only laughed and said, "Haven't you ever seen a wet vet before?"

Chapter 7

One incident from the town of Wilton remains strongly etched in my memory. I was testing the herd of Joe Donovan, who was either a devout Catholic or a passionate Protestant. There were six little children under the age of 10 watching me in the barn. Their mother had delivered a new baby several days earlier and, was still in the hospital.

I had finished with the cows that were stanchioned, and only a bull remained in that part of the barn as we drove the cows out. He had a ring in his nose, which was chained to a wall. I went to a wing of the barn to inject some heifers and was having some problems with one who did not want to be touched. Finally I'd had enough, and got a rope to slow her down. When she hit the end of that she fell down with a long bellow and the next thing I knew, there was the bull, with his nose ripped out, and blood flowing over his face. I was cornered with no place to go, and if he had not stopped to attack a manure carrier this story might never have been written. The children were scrambling up walls to get out of the way, and I yelled, "Open the barn door and let him out"

Joe responded, "We will never catch him if we do. We have to tie him up". I was not all anxious to argue with a bleeding, mad bull that weighed over a thousand pounds, but I knew he was right. So armed with a length of pipe, I faced him and stood my ground. I planned to break his leg if I had to, but fortunately for both of us, he went to a stanchion and we secured him with at length of hayfork rope. He had been close enough to me that my coveralls were covered with blood, which fortunately, was his. The next day he went to Burger King to the other side of the counter. He did not get his TB test.

Early on a Monday morning, the week before we were to be married, I was traveling down a hilly, crooked road when a large car came around a curve on my side of the road. I veered to the right and missed him, but when I tried to pull back, the car skidded, went into deep ditch and rolled on its top. The County highway department had dumped huge boulders in to slow erosion and the roof was crushed. I crawled out the window, climbed up the side of the ditch and walked to a nearby farm to call a sheriff's department. The accident had already been reported. It must have been the driver of the other car, who hadn't bothered to stop. My mother had given my brother Jerry and me $500 to purchase two cars or one. We had decided to buy a 1951 Ford and share it. I could see most of the summer's work going to pay for a new car. The Ford dealer in Tomah hauled our car back to the garage, and I called my bride to be to tell her what happened, and to I assure her that I was fine. I put it off as long as I could, but I had to make the call that I dreaded most. I called my dad and told him, and got a strong lecture on safe driving. Then the good news; he told me he knew it would happen and he had taken out collision insurance.

Chapter 8

We had finally reached our junior year and were permitted, no, required to go across the street to the Stange Memorial Clinic for part of the day. We still had some classes in the Quadrangle. We had Infectious Diseases with Dean Merchant, Special Pathology with Dr. Frank Ramsey, and Practical Anatomy with John Balm. Dr. Merchant wore two hats. When he was a teacher, he was an all-right fellow, but when he was acting as the Dean, he could be as tough as nails. I was never called to his office, but his secretary was the wife of one of my classmates and we would occasionally get the lowdown. One of the fellows had taken a coed to a dance at his fraternity. At the end of the evening he asked her if she wanted to go home and she replied, "Please take me. I live in California. " They both thought did would be a big joke on her parents, but they did not see the humor in it and immediately put her on a plane back to Iowa. He had to drive back alone and ran into a blizzard in Montana and missed four days of class. He was called to the dean's office, and lectured on the seriousness of taking a girl across state lines for immoral purposes. Bob cried and told the dean, "I never touched her!"

Dr. Ramsey was the finest teacher I ever had in college. He was the first to take a personal interest in me, and tried to help rather than harass. He had been a high school teacher before becoming a veterinarian. He was tall and thin, in his fifties, and was always pleasant. We took all our lecture notes in bound books and one day to emphasize a point, he jumped up on the desk, put his foot in the wastepaper basket, and told us write this in capital letters across two pages: "There is no post-mortem hemorrhage." Needless to say it, made an impression. However on rare occasions, some one would describe the lesion as post-mortem bleeding and he would hit the roof.

There were two classrooms in the Clinic, where we took Obstetrics with Dr. Emerson and Dr. Rueber, a horny, single Canadian who would constantly make remarks to the married fellows, which were not appreciated. Bob McClure was the youngest of the class and lived in a fraternity. He started dating his housemother, who was at least 12 years older than him. A big problem arose when Dr. Rueber started dating the same woman. Bob got a "D" in Obstetrics, and had to drop out for a year. During that time he took more Anatomy classes, and when he graduated he had a Master's degree. He went on to become a professor of Anatomy at Cornell and University of Missouri, and never did practice veterinary medicine, but we always considered him a member of our class. He married Betty, and they lived together for many years until their divorce.

Chapter 9

During the spring quarter of my junior year I decided I wanted to work in the summer with a practicing veterinarian and get some firsthand experience. I believed that my qualifications as a tuberculosis tester was my best hope to getting a job, and so I inquired from the Wisconsin Department of the Agriculture which counties were to be tested. I then checked the AVMA directory and wrote to the veterinarians in them, telling of my qualifications and asking for work. Lacrosse County was one of them, and had only two large animal practitioners. Dr. Robert Hauser replied to my letter, and we set up an interview during Easter break.

The Lacrosse clinic was located about 3 miles from the city. It was a two-story stucco building with the office, clinic and kennels on the first floor. The living quarters were above. I had no idea what to expect when I knocked on the stairway door. A very large man was lying on a couch covered with a blanket, and a small woman nearby. He had recently had an appendectomy and the incision had become infected. He appeared to have an extremely large abdomen and weighed nearly 300 lbs. With all that abdominal fat, it was no wonder it had not healed properly.

We chatted for a few minutes, discussing large animal veterinary medicine and my experience working for the state. He told me that he had a large number of herds to be tested for both tuberculosis and brucellocis. He asked me what I expected to be paid. I told them I was looking for experience, and I was ready to work for what he thought was fair. He looked at me and said, "I thought you fellows had that all figured out before you left school." He said he would pay me hundred dollars a week plus car expenses, and I nearly fell off the chair. It was much more than I had expected.

Years later his wife, Opal, told me she had threatened to leave him if he didn't hire the first fellow that walked through the door. That first day she asked," Can you kill dogs?" They kept the stray dogs from a couple of townships and their kennels were full. We went downstairs and proceeded to eliminate their problem. It was the start of a long and deep relationship that has lasted over 50 years.

School was out on the seventh of June, and on the eighth, Olive and I were in Lacrosse. The ladies immediately became fast friends, as both were nurses. It turned out that Opal was the daughter of the farmer, Oswald Schnek, who I had met the previous summer in Hickston. The Hausers had been married shortly after graduation ten years previously, and had two small boys, Jay and Bill. Doc was nine years older than I, as he had finished vet school at Iowa State in three years. They had built the clinic on his dad's farm and his sister and husband and family still lived in the old farmhouse next door. They had not had a vacation since their honeymoon, and so the next weekend they took the boys and left, while we moved into the apartment and took over the practice for three days. Talk about learning to swim when you fallout of the boat! That's nothing compared to taking over a veterinary practice after three years of school!

Lacrosse County lies along the Mississippi River, and is consequently very hilly. The countryside is filled with bluffs and valleys. Their roads are trails made by drunken Indians. They either run on top of the ridges or through the valleys, which are called coulies, and are not necessarily joined directly. Sometimes you have to drive miles in order to get from one to the other. The farms were located either along the ridge or up a coulie. It was said that the cows had short legs on one side in order to walk along the sides of a hill.

It was nothing to drive 60 miles to test 10 herds. Dr. Hauser's practice covered the larger part of the county and extended across the river into Minnesota. He was very well liked and respected, and consequently his clients readily accepted me. I never told them I was a Doctor, but likewise, I didn't advertise myself as a student. I would usually test cattle during the morning hours and spend the afternoon in the office, except during those times when he was gone and I was responsible for the calls. I had hoped to spend time with him and learn by watching and listening. It didn't work out that way. During the entire summer I spent one afternoon on calls with him.

In the clinic, I would treat small animals, giving inoculations for rabies and distemper. I would also treat sick animals giving shots and dispensing medications. He had never encouraged the small animal practice because he had been too busy to give it proper attention. He chastised me one day for the way I was building it up because when I was gone the people were going to be disappointed. I also took care of the boarding dogs; keeping them fed and watered, and the kennels cleaned.

Before long, I was meeting with the drug salesmen, and ordered the biologics and antibiotics. When we were in school, we had no idea of the cost for them. One, which we used a great deal, was Terramycin and when the Pfizer man came I ordered 10 bottles. Dr. Hauser asked if I really like that drug and was it used to a lot at school? It seemed I had spent $850 for it. We returned nine bottles.

Before the summer was over, Doc and Opal left us with the kids and the practice for an entire week. We moved into the house and accepted the responsibility. A couple of cases remained vividly in my mind. I was called to Minnesota to treat a sick horse. Horses were not, and still are not a strong point of mine. It was a work horse, standing and weaving with its eyes half closed in a stall. It looked like just a sick horse to me, but the farmer thought it had sleeping sickness because he had another one like it several years earlier. I told him I agreed completely and I would treat the horse for it. I ordered the medicine and injected the animal when it came, and fortunately for all, it recovered. I was called to deliver a calf from a small heifer. There was no way to get it without doing an embryotomy. I had to cut up the calf inside the cow and deliver the pieces. The parts weighed 160 pounds, and I weighed 145 pounds.

Chapter 10

After working in the field as practicing veterinarians, we began to realize that our teachers had been lying to us. Clients did not need to know the anatomy of the stay apparatus in a horse, nor were they interested that the Indian Rice Rat had a placenta attachment unique to itself. They wanted to know only three things: what's wrong, can you fix it, and how much will it cost?

As seniors, we spent the entire day in the clinic. Our professors were Baker and Jensen for Small Animal Medicine, Covalt and Simpson for Small Animal Surgery, Fowler and Whitcomb for Large Animal Surgery, Kingery for Large Animal Medicine, Monlux for Post-Mortem, Yoder with the State Diagnostic Lab, Margaret Sloss, the only woman on the staff, for Clinical Pathology, and Chivers and Lundvall for Ambulatory. Each one of these doctors was a character unto him or her self, but I will only tell of three or four incidents.

We would spend one week upstairs with the small animals and the next one downstairs in the barn. One of my classmates wanted only to graduate and spend the rest of his life vaccinating hogs for cholera. He had no time for small animals and would sneak out every possible opportunity, and go downstairs to the barn. Fate would have it that when he entered the Army, he was stationed at Walter Reed Hospital caring for the lab animals. His entire career as a veterinarian was in laboratory animals and he never vaccinated a hog in 50 years.

Dr. Lundvall was a tall, easygoing individual who had not been blessed with an overabundance of ambition. We were assigned one week each quarter on Ambulatory where we would go to the farms and work under his supervision. We were vaccinating pigs one day, a process that required us to catch them and hold them up by their front legs while Dr. Lundvall handled the syringe. One of my classmates, a farm boy, stated he had gone to college for seven years to get on the other side of the pig with the syringe!

The call I remember most vividly was the one in which we were to dehorn some stocker beef cattle outside of town. We had to stop and have a coffee before we could continue with the cattle chute. We had run the first animal into the chute and had him firmly secured when Dr. Lundvall produced a new electric dehorning saw. "Now men, I will demonstrate, but you must be very careful as this saw is very fast and with that he cut off one horn as well as the ear."

The farmer yelled, "Judas priest, Doc. You cut off his ear!" Without missing a beat, Lundvall repeated, "I tell you men, this machine is very fast," and proceeded to cut off the other ear along with the horn. Now the farmer really yelled, and the doctor calmly said, "This saw it is too fast and we will put it away and use a hand saw." There were three of us students watching and holding our breath to keep from laughing, for we knew that our chances of graduating hung in the balance.

Chapter 11

The school year 1954-55 was a most stressful year of my life; not because of school, although that added to the problems, but the things that were happening in my personal life.

My mother had developed heart problems in 1953. Her heart was not receiving enough circulation and consequently, it would slow down to the point that her brain was not getting enough oxygen, and she would black out if she did any strenuous activity. She had to quit going to the barn or doing any chores. My brother Jerry dropped out of college and came home to help. She did very little for about eight months and when she was reexamined by the doctors, she was told she was much better, and to continue doing nothing. She knew better and was determined not to live the rest of her life in that fashion. She insisted that Jerry go back to college in September. She went back to work on the farm and in October, suffered a fatal heart attack. I drove all night from Iowa and got home just in time to hear that she had died in hospital.

My grandfather Crawley had committed suicide by carbon monoxide when he was 50 years old, and ever since I was eight or nine, if my father was missing, I was sent to find him. So the first thing I did that morning was to take all the guns apart and hide the pieces. Sure enough, he started talking about having a double funeral. He went to bed that day and got up only for the funeral. I had to make all the arrangements, including selecting the coffin, her burial clothes and the pallbearers.

The night of the wake was a horrible nightmare. The day after the funeral, he disappeared. I called and called for him, until I found him lying upstairs in the haymow, and then I blew up. I told him how selfish he was, and if he ever did that to me again he wouldn't have to commit suicide because I would kill him. Jerry quit college again and came home, and he told me for the next couple of months, Dad would take a gunnysack and lie crying on Mother's grave.

In December, Jerry appeared at our door in Ames and told me he had had to move out. Dad was accusing him of mother's death and said he was going to kill him. I talked to several doctors, and they all said he had to be hospitalized in a mental institution. And so, during Christmas vacation, I went to a county judge and swore out the proper papers. It was the morning of the last day of the year when the deputy sheriffs came, and took him away in a straitjacket to Mendota state hospital in Madison. I think that was worse than the day they buried mother.

My aunts and uncles both sides condemned me for what I had done. Only my mother's sister Ethel and her husband Bill stood behind me, and from that day forward, I had very little to do with the rest . When I needed them, they were gone, and now I could get along without them.

I made several trips to Madison to visit but he refused to see me. I refused to sign the papers for his release until they were sure he was well. The doctors told me he hated me, and I was never to offer any advice to him again.

Meanwhile, Olive had suffered two miscarriages in the first trimester of her pregnancies and we were unsure what God had in mind for us.

Two weeks before graduation, I got a phone call that Uncle Bill had been killed in a plane crash. Since Aunt Ethel was alone, I went back to help her.

Without the love and support of my wife and my faith in God, I don't think I would have survived.

Chapter 12

Dr. Chivers was a tall and thin old man, with sparse, white hair and glasses. He was slightly stooped and walked very slowly and talked even slower. It was hard to imagine that he had graduated with the highest grades in the history of the college. "Hurry" and "worry" were not words in his vocabulary. My first encounter with him occurred during my junior year, when a senior student and I were assigned to treat an adult female Angus cow, who wanted no part of us, or rather all of us. She would charge us every time we tried to get into the pen, and you don't fool around with such an animal. When a bull charges, he has his head down, and you can jump aside if you are quick enough. When a cow charges, she comes at you head-up, and there is no way to elude them.

Dr. Chivers observed her for some time, then turned and asked the senior, "Have you ever shot a cow?" The student replied, "I have given lots of shots to cows." Dr. Chivers smiled and went to his office, and when he returned he had a shotgun, which he handed to the student and said, "Shoot her."

As a senior student, I was assigned to take care of an old Guernsey cow, and while my to juniors were moving her, she fell. They got an electric prod to get her up, but she had a heart attack and died. I was fearful of the consequences when I told Dr. Chivers, but he laughed and said, "That cow was not worth a barrel full of sour owl shit!" I guess that is the epitome of worthlessness.

Dr. Brunell Kingery taught Large Animal Medicine, and was very respected and admired by all of us. He was the only a professor on the staff will had been a successful practicing veterinarian. The rest of them had never left the hallowed halls of Ivy, so we listened to him and felt he knew what he was talking about. He received a PhD, and later became the Dean of Kansas State Veterinary College.

The administration of ISU were convinced that the road to hell was paved with Pabst beer cans. To be caught drinking was grounds for expulsion. This rule caused a lot of dissension in the class, as we were all over 24 years of age, and a half had had military experience. To be told you can't have a drink went down pretty hard. Doctors Whitcomb and Payne a chaperoned a couple of affairs, but when the dean heard there had been alcohol, they were relieved of all future duties and he showed up with his steely eyes.

For four long years we all yearned for graduation day, but when it arrived, it was a bittersweet occasion as we began to realize that these fast friends would each go their separate ways and we might never see them again. When you have been through hell and high water, you form a kinship which is hard to break. There were 57 of us that walked across the stage in June of 1955. 34 are now deceased, and last summer 28 of us got together for a reunion. Six of us were commissioned First Lieutenant in the Air Force, while 18 went into the army. There was no rhyme nor reason as to the difference, but I always looked better in blue.

Section Two: The Air Force

Chapter 13

It took two long days of hard driving, pulling the house trailer, to reach Montgomery, Alabama from Lacrosse, Wisconsin. I signed in on August 13th at Gunter Air Force Base, which was to be our home for the next six weeks. My military career had begun. This was merely a training base and there were no planes. Although one morning there was 10 to 15 dirigibles moored on the runways, having been evacuated from the coast because of hurricanes.

The first two weeks was called BMOC, which meant Basic Medical Orientation Course for medical doctors, dentists, veterinarians and nurses. We were all handled with kid gloves by Captain Chapman. He answered to our every need and every time we turned around we were given more money. After living hand to mouth as students, we were sure we had reached the Promised Land. There were uniform allowances, quarters allowances, substance pay and temporary duty allotments. The checks never seemed to cease; we were in hog heaven. Besides, the Officers' Club had happy hour every afternoon at 4 when we had two drinks for the price of one. There were three of my classmates who had received Air Force commissions there also. At the end of the session we were to march in review for the base commander, and since I was one of the few who had had a smattering of military training, I was appointed the platoon leader. If ever there were a group of intelligent people with two left feet, they were behind me. Montgomery was also the home of Maxwell Air Force Base, which is the war college of the Air Force and there was a large contingent of Air Force personnel stationed there. We had been instructed to look up a Sergeant Merrill Bates, a farm boy from Iowa stationed there and soon-to-be discharged. He and his wife and their small son were great people and we got along famously. They needed furniture and he had an Allstate motor scooter, so we made a trade.

We took the bedroom set from the trailer replaced it with a hide-a-bed and left with a motor scooter.

The next four weeks were spent in VMOC, Veterinary Medical Orientation Course. Not all of them had been in ROTC and this was new stuff for them. We learned how to fill out medical forms concerning our duties as veterinarians, we went on field trips to learn inspection procedures, and the four weeks went by in flash.

Olive was reminded she was in the Deep South before the days of Rosa Parks when she tried to hail a cab and the colored driver told her, "I'm sorry lady I can't haul white folks." The only other thing that comes to my mind from Montgomery is Shinbaum's Clothing Store. We were obliged to have an officer's mess dress uniform. I had one tailored and to this day it is the most expensive piece of clothing I own. It ceased to fit me years ago but I can't bear to part with it.

John E. Crawley, DVM

Chapter 14

Hunter Air Force Base was located in Savannah, Georgia, and was one of the very few that was named for a living Air Force pilot. It was the home of the 38th Air Division, composed of 308th and 2nd Bomb Wings with their air refueling groups, and 4231st air base group. We belonged to SAC (Strategic Air Command) under leadership of General Curtis Le May, who had convinced Congress and the world we were the only thing preventing total annihilation. We received the bulk of the Air Force budget and it filtered down even to my office. All of our planes were B-47 bombers, armed with nuclear weapons. Our base was very security conscious and frequently had a base alert to deter penetration teams from other SAC bases. We were in the midst of such an exercise the day I arrived, and I was subject to much scrutiny. Each of the Bomb Wings was structured to act independently when deployed overseas. They would send the entire Wing and its supporting personnel to North Africa for a period of 90 days TDY (Temporary Duty assignment). I was assigned to the 308th, but since there had not then a Base Veterinarian in nearly two years, they reassigned me to in the 4231st Air Base Group, under the command of Colonel Blakey. The Hospital Commander was Colonel Gerald Long, and they were the only two people I had to take orders from. As long as I kept them happy, there was no sweat.

I soon found out that what you knew didn't matter nearly as much as who you knew. The TO (Table of Organization) called for one veterinarian and four enlisted men for each wing. I had two, and when I complained to Major Thomas, the second Air Force veterinarian, I was told live with it. The Veterinary Corps is composed of officers only, and the enlisted personnel are trained medical, and under the command of a hospital officer. They were my responsibility only while on duty during the day. My main duties were food inspections and providing medical support for the sentry guard dogs. There were nine different classes of food inspection, and

I was to make monthly reports on the pounds of food inspected in each class. One such class was "prior to purchase". The Army Quartermaster Corps issued the contracts for these, and we had one for frozen breaded shrimp. I had been there for a few weeks when an IG (Inspector General), an Army colonel veterinarian came to call. I took him to the shrimp plant in Thunderbolt where one of my men was working, and then to the locker plant in downtown Savannah where the other man supervised their storage. He was completely satisfied with our performance but when he asked me about the rest of our food inspections and reports, I told him it was mainly a figment of my imagination. He gasped, and looked at me in amazement. I said I was not going to lie, as he could plainly see where my two men were working and who would be available to do the other inspections. He returned to Washington and reported to USAF, and that's when the fecal matter hit the oscillating mechanism! I received a call from Major Thomas who asked, "What the hell did you tell that IG?" He had just been chewed out by Colonel Snodgrass, SAC Veterinarian, who had been chastised from Washington. I certainly got their attention!

Chapter 15

It is SOP (Standard Operating Procedure) when you have a VIP (Very Important Person), you are to introduce them to the Base Commander and your immediate commanders, and so I took the Army IG to visit Colonel Blakey. After the proper introductions, the colonel turned to me and asked, "How is your wife, and have you had that baby?" The next stop was the Hospital Surgeon office and again, after introductions, Colonel Long inquired about Olive and the birth to be. The last straw was broken when we visited the Air Force veterinarian stationed at Paris Island Marine Base, and he asked if the baby had arrived yet. At this point, the visiting Colonel commented, "Is this the first baby to be born in the Air Force?"

In the following month I was assigned four new vet technicians, including a tech sergeant from MacDill Air Force who was experienced in shrimp inspection. The hospital sent me a clerk typist and a truck driver, so suddenly I had nearly a full complement of personnel and I could run the base veterinary office in the manner in which it was intended. The men were all cross-trained so they could rotate responsibilities every two months, and not become careless or bored. I had been instructed when I arrived to provide all the small animal support I could to keep the Air Force personnel as happy as possible. Consequently, Wednesday afternoons were set aside for surgery and Friday mornings was for sick call. One man was designated to help in the clinic. I told them if I got bit or scratched, they would lose one stripe. During the next two years, no one was ever demoted.

In order to keep a closer account of the food entering the base, we issued gate passes to every truck, which had to be stamped by our office before they could leave. We also stamped their invoices so they could be paid. With these practices in place, we had pretty firm control. We had a long list orphansof businesses that were approved to to sell to the military. Our personnel inspected all periodically.

Depending on the food supplied; dairies, fish and meat markets and bakeries were checked once a month. Others that handled only packaged goods with little chance of contamination would go two to three months.

To be removed from the approved list had serious consequences for a vendor. The pop bottling plants originally were not inspected, but a sergeant told us of finding a worm in a bottle. When he returned it to the plant, the manager dropped the bottle and said, "What worm?" It was time for action, and we changed their mind in a hurry. On another occasion, I was inspecting an ice producing facility that did not want to provide adequate bathroom facilities for the colored help, and had decided they didn't need to be on the list. When we called some of our other suppliers, such as the Frank Mathews Fish Market, and told them they would have to get a different ice source to remain approved, the bathrooms were installed. We found out the time and time again you could not depend on the city Health Department to do the job.

Chapter 16

The PM (Preventive Medicine) Department shared our office building, and was staffed by a young shave tail by the name of Lt. Jerome Premack, who had graduated from a small eastern Catholic university, an Airman Cooper and a Sergeant Aldrige. Our command styles differed greatly. With his gold bar he demanded respect, and expected to be saluted each time he entered the building. My manner was much different and more casual. I was called "Doc", and tried to earn respect. His troops and the rest of the office personnel would derisively refer to him as "Junior" behind his back. On one occasion I received an urgent phone call from the office during the noon hour to hurry back, as Airman Wagner was going to kill Junior. Wagner had transferred from the Army to the Air Force, but since he could neither read nor write he could not be classified. They sent him to me to be used as a truck driver, which worked well as long as he could go to someplace he knew and not have to read street signs. He was a rather large fellow, and set in his ways. The lieutenant wanted him to drive out to the sanitary field, but Wagner insisted it was his lunchtime, and he didn't have to go. When he gave him a direct order and Wagner still refused, he threatened a court-martial. This is when things became hot and heavy, and my first sergeant decided they needed Doc. I separated them, and brought each to my office, and calmed the waters.

Our base was very security conscious and along with the SAC penetrations we also had exercises involving the OSI (Operations Security Investigation). One morning Sergeant Aldrige came into my office and said, "Junior is getting his tit in the wringer." It seemed that a major from Second Air Force had arrived to check the blueprints for the base water supply and Junior was giving them to him. The sergeant was very suspicious, and when we contacted Base Operations, there had been no flights in from Barksdale and none were scheduled out. By the time we had discovered the ruse the damage had been done. A couple of months later, I met the fellow at the Base Exchange. When I asked him how his water works were, he just smiled. We did sponsor a bowling team to compete in the base league, with black shirts and gold lettering of "PM and Vets" embroidered on the back.

When airman Cooper, who was an Oklahoma Indian, decided to get married to a local gal, he honored me by asking me to be his best man. It was the first time I had ever been in a Baptist Church with its huge baptismal tank. Fortunately all us had been baptized previously.

Chapter 17

Our stay at Hunter Air Force Base might have been much shorter if a certain lady had not been broad minded and forgiving. Shortly after our arrival, I was performing surgery one Wednesday morning when the sergeant knocked on the door and said, "Some lady is on the phone with a tick in the dog's nipple."

"Tell her to put some fingernail polish remover on it and gently remove it." I thought anyone who lived in the South would know enough to remove a tick. On Friday morning during the weekly sick call, a woman appeared with a middle-aged springer spaniel bitch, and when she announced she had been the lady who had called about the tick, the chip on my shoulder grew larger. Upon examining the dog, I found it had an inverted nipple, which had been there since birth, and so I pointedly remarked she must not have paid much attention to the dog. She told me the animal belonged to her daughter, who had just left for college. There was a small charge for each animal seen and as she was leaving, I told her that would be "50 cents please". She apologized and left but by this time the entire office was aghast. "Don't you know who that was?" they inquired, and I shook my head no. "That was the general's wife. Didn't you see the staff car with the flag?" But the damage had already been done. That afternoon at the Officers' Club, the new wives were introduced to her, and when she met Olive as the new Base Veterinarian's wife she remarked, "Oh yes, I met him this morning."

During the next couple of years, I had occasion to see her several times when she brought the dog in and we became friends, but I always treated her with a great deal of respect.As Base Veterinarian, I was in a position to do favors for various people: the First Sergeant of the Motor Pool, the crash boat crew, Base Supply Officer, and the Base Exchange Official. I had always wanted to own a new shotgun and so one day I went to the Base Exchange to purchase one. I was familiar with full and modified chokes, but had never seen improved cylinder, and when I inquired of the clerk she referred me to Charles Bennett, the manager, who was quite a hunter in his own right. He asked me what I intended to hunt and when I replied pheasants, he recommended the improved cylinder. He told me he would order the gun in his name so the Base Exchange would not get their commission and when the salesman came, he put the gun in his name as a favor to Charles. I ended up paying $87 for a new Remington pump shotgun.

Mr. Bennett invited me to go deer hunting on his brothers' ranch in central Georgia, and so it was I found myself seated on the stump in the middle of a Palmetto swamp early one morning in November. I had been placed there and threatened with bodily harm if I should move. These boys were real Georgia crackers and not to be fooled with. They had cut the shirttail off Charles because he missed a deer a couple of weeks earlier. So I watched and waited and listened for the dogs. As they drew nearer I could hear the crashing of the deer and I vowed they weren't going to get my shirttail. At 20 yards I leveled on a six-point buck with a load of buckshot, blowing out his heart and breaking both front legs. I made the big mistake of admitting it was my first deer and got initiated by having my face and hair covered with blood. At the dinner table their grandmother remarked. "Looks like Dr. got a deer."

Chapter 18

Following the old adage that "the ends justify the means" almost got me in big trouble. Any drugs or medicines I could not get from a hospital, I purchased through non-appropriated funds, and any moneys we received in the office was to be paid to them. There were some expenses and equipment we did not have funds for, so a slush fund was established. We charged $2.50 for small animal operations. I calculated we used 70 cents of government material, and the rest was the result of my labor and consequently was ours to be used as we wished to. We also boarded dogs for the base personnel, and any profit was fair game for the fund. I had established a "cussing can"; whenever anyone used profanity, it cost them a nickel. This also went into the cigar box in the safe, under the supervision of Sergeant Pierce.

Every Saturday morning we were subject to inspection by hospital personnel, which included the lawn. We found it necessary to purchase a lawn mower and a floor scrubber/waxer, which were paid for by the slush fund. The bowling shirts and part of the bowling fees also came out of there. We had a couple of office picnics for the men and their families, all for esprit de corps. It also served as a short-term loan office. They could borrow up to $20 for 10 days. No moneys were ever spent on individuals, however I was suspicious that the radio they gave me upon discharge came from it.

Sometime after I left, the Hospital Adjutant came to the office and searched the safe. When he found the cigar box and the account book, the fecal matter hit the oscillating mechanism. He called for a board of inquiry to investigate the entire matter. Each and every person in the office was called to testify in secret about the fund and me. They tried to recall me to active duty to face charges, but I checked with the JAG (Judge Advocate General) at Truax Field, and they advised me to ignore the entire matter. However, I believe Sergeant Pierce got stuck for three hundred dollars. I did receive a copy of the testimony by each of my men, and was very gratified for the loyalty and respect they professed for me.

The Hospital Troop Commander, Lt. Joe Kehoe, and I became very close personal friends. My office became a dumping ground for personnel problems at the hospital, because I had the time and inclination to work with those troops. They were warned I was their last hope to stay in the Air Force. This was how I acquired Wagner, the truck driver; Derroso, a clerk typist; Dellano, the lab tech; and one other, who reported to our office with a broken jaw from fighting. He went AWOL for a week on me, and when I admitted failure to Joe, he told me they were lucky at the hospital if he was there a week. Sometimes there are good reasons young man get in trouble; such was the case with the Delando. He had suffered a scar in his youth that drew his mouth into a sneer and consequently, people treated him with contempt. If he didn't have to face people, he got along fine, and I arranged his duties to protect him as best I could.

Chapter 19

When I returned back to the trailer the second day of work, I was greeted by a very beautiful, pregnant wife with tears in her eyes who said, "I want to go home." The trailer was parked just outside the base in the midst of about 15 others, with no shade and sewage seeping from the ground. It was very obvious that some changes had to be made if my happy home life was to continue. We visited three or four other trailer parks near the base, but all of them left a great deal to be desired.

We finally stopped at a small place called "Friend Field". It was about ten acres in size, away from the road and containing a large house and seven trailers. The lawn was well kept, with numerous flower gardens surrounded by massive water oaks draped with long strands of Spanish moss. It appeared to be everything we had hoped for, but when I knocked on the door, I was greeted by a middle-aged overweight Southern lady who informed me they had no room but I could put my name on a long list of applicants. I told her I would like to do that and my name was Dr. Crawley. Her attitude immediately changed and she said, "Oh, Doctor is it?" and smiled broadly. We had noticed a white-haired old gentleman working on the lawn as we drove in and I had assumed he was a gardener, but now she opened the door and called out, "Stanley, come here and meet Doctor Crawley and his lovely wife."

He studied me closely for a while, and then asked, "Do you know how to work?" I assured him that was my middle name, and he said, "We'll find out." It seemed one of the tenets was TDY for several weeks and their spot was open, so we could use it until I had prepared a new place for our trailer. We moved the very next day, and I began to trench the water system and construct a sanitary field and pour a cement patio. I was grateful and appreciative for the opportunity to live there and I tried to help maintain the park.

The rest of the residents were all Air Force personnel and he was disdainful of them. He thought all military people were parasites on society and was not averse to letting you know. He had once been a successful and wealthy masonry contractor who had built large edifices in Savannah, but had lost most of his money in the crash of 1929. They had had a large estate with servants and a gardener, but now it was just him and Mrs. Watson. He informed me he was a colonel and when I asked what branch of service, he said it was an honorary title but couldn't tell me who bestowed it. We got along quite well but only because I worked to help him. Every Sunday morning would find him working all around our trailer while I ate breakfast and drank coffee. One day he inquired why I didn't help him on Sundays and I said it was a day of rest. He told me, "The good Lord said if your ox falls in the ditch on Sunday, you can pull him out." When I replied, "Mr. Watson, your ox falls in every Sunday", he stomped away.

Mrs. Watson was very prejudiced and was quick to show it. One day one of the wives asked where she could hire a colored lady, and was told, "There are colored women or girls, but ladies are all white." Another time, one of the wives offered a piece of candy to the house cleaner and she was chastised that, "You do not offer them a choice. You hand it to them." When they occasionally hired an old black gardener, she made him ride in the trunk of her 1938 Chevy, holding the lid on his head. I once asked Mr. Watson why they let these people raise their children, cook their food and live with them and treat them the way they do. He said, "Doctor, down south we'd don't care how close they get, as long as they don't get too high. Up north, you don't care how high they get to, as long as they don't get too close."

John E. Crawley, DVM

Chapter 20

One of my main responsibilities as Base Veterinarian was the care and supervision of the sentry dog program. When I first arrived, there were 12 dogs, but in the intervening two years, that had grown to 48. They were all German Shepherds and males with one exception. She was known as "Mitch the bitch". Each dog was assigned one handler who took care of the animal, and worked as a team when on duty. They worked only at night and in locations where no one else was supposed to be. They would all alert to the presence of intruders up to a distance of one half mile. They were housed in steel kennels away from the rest of the base and were transported to their duty stations each evening by truck. They hated one another as much as people, and I was called upon frequently to suture bite wounds they received while on the truck. Since they were used only at night and we were located in the midst of saltwater marshes, mosquitos were a large problem. They transmitted a parasite known as heartworms, which were located in the chambers of the heart and could cause death. Each month I would conduct a blood test on each animal to diagnose infections. Positive dogs were treated by intravenous injections of an arsenic compound for 10 consecutive days. It was a very corrosive substance and one drop outside the vein would cause a slough of the flesh. This was in the days before heartworm prevention, so you could return a treated dog to duty and have it re-infected within a week. I tried to develop some substance to repel the mosquitos from the dog, without success. We soon found out that 6-12, a repellent for humans, put the dogs out of commission for the rest of the night if they licked it.

When the dogs were brought to the clinic, they were always accompanied by the handler and muzzled, as they had no great love for me. On one occasion the largest dog of the group -- Samson, by name, was waiting outside on the porch. A sergeant who had been over-served at the NCO club came by and decided to pat the nice dog. Fortunately for him, he had no idea what he was dealing with, and showed no fear nor hesitation. The dog was completely nonplused and did not attack, but the handler holding the dog needed a change of underwear.

I was invited to a veterinary conference for Second Army vets at Fort McPherson to speak about the care and problems of the sentry dog program. The Air Force had previously sent me to Fort Carson Colorado, where all sentry dogs were purchased and trained by the army. I came away feeling guilty because they had over four hundred dogs, and I had more supplies and equipment for my 28 animals. The sky was the limit when it came to supporting the SAC dog program, and I admit I took full advantage of the opportunities.

Chapter 21

I was home eating lunch when I got an urgent message from one of my troops: "Doc, you better get back here right away. I think we have a big problem." The truck driver from the Wilson Packing Co. had brought in his invoices to be stamped, and across one was written, "Deliver this before stopping at the vet office." It was very obvious that something was amiss. The invoice was for chickens to be delivered to the NC0 Club, and upon examining them, they were not USDA inspected. I had been observing a poultry processing plant and had seen first-hand the difference between the inspected and un-inspected birds. The chickens are sorted before slaughter, and any sickly ones go on the un-inspected line. They are processed with less care and consequently, USDA birds command a higher price. It seemed that the salesman from Wilson and the sergeant from the NC0 Club had agreed to use the cheaper birds, even though they were fully aware of the illegality of such action. I reported the violation to the Base Commander, Colonel Blakey, and the salesman and the sergeant were both terminated, and Wilson Packing was removed from the approved list and could not sell anything to the armed forces for a period of six months. My actions only improved my standing with the Base Commander.

In April of 1956, I found myself in Oak Ridge Tennessee, attending a two-week course on radiological warfare, along with 20 other Air Force veterinarians. Needless to say, this information was of little value during my 50 years as a practicing vet. I had been appointed CBR (Chemical Biological Radiological) Officer for the hospital. I served only once in this capacity. A nationwide exercise called "War Dance" was held that summer. I reported to an underground bombproof bunker to await the news of where the atomic bomb had been dropped in our area. We were to assess the damage to our base and determine how soon we could become operational again. When the news came, they had dropped the bomb in the middle of Savannah, but it was a hydrogen bomb. We searched top secret manuals to determine the area of destruction, and it seemed we had all been removed from the face of the earth. Our part of the exercise was over.

I had one last occasion to stir the pot and make waves. Second Air Force ordered me to supply two vet technicians for a six months in Los Alamos testing ground. When I complained to the Hospital Adjutant that this would cripple my office, he replied that there was nothing he could do. I went to the Base Commander and told him of my plight, and he responded, "They can't do that to us." I said we could supply one if necessary, but certainly not two for that long a time. He immediately got on the phone and informed Second Air Force that would be the case, and the orders were remanded. When the Hospital Adjutant found out what had happened, he questioned me as to what I had done. I told him, "You said you could do nothing, so I went to someone who could." He was very distressed that I had gone over his head, and told me never asked me for anything again. I assured him I wouldn't, as I was to be discharged in less than a month.

Chapter 22

I first met Kelly as a patient when he was presented in my office at Hunter Air Force Base for inoculations. A young woman and her mother brought her in, and I was immediately greatly impressed by the dog. It was not only his appearance, as he stood about 32 in. at the shoulder and weighed nearly 75 lbs. He had large yellow eyes characteristic of his breed, but his color was sable and looked like burnished leather. But what impressed me most was a look in his eye, which told me he was a very intelligent animal. Over the years my first impression was proven right time and time again. I told the owners they were very fortunate to have such a dog.

Upon examining him I could tell life to that point had been tough; there was a white line around his muzzle, which indicated that if it had been wired shut. He was only about 6 months old and was already on his fourth owner. He had originally come from the East Coast and had been bred by Arthur Godfrey, who gave or sold him to someone in that area who mistreated him because of his barking. He ended up in New Orleans with the mother, and now she had brought him to Savannah for her daughter and family.

The Weimaraner breed was developed in Germany in the 1900's by the count of Weimer for hunting deer and large game, but was later used mainly for bird hunting. It was the result of mating a German Shorthaired Pointer and some other breeds. They refuse to disclose the other breeds because they didn't want their results to be duplicated so to this day the cross is unknown. The dogs, known as gray ghosts, were not for sale for love or money, but after the war the Germans were not in a position to prevent their exportation to the states. They were still very rare and commanded a price of between $1,200 to $2,000 a piece, and soon the Americans began to breed them indiscriminately, mating litter mates, fathers and daughters, sons and mothers, and consequently producing animals with genetic defects. When I was in college, I remarked to one of the doctors we had a large number of Weimaraners in a hospital, considering they were rare and he told me most were there because of genetic abnormalities. It had taken the Germans over 100 years to develop the breed, and it had taken the Americans 10 years to destroy it. Kelly was the result of such a meeting, and consequently reverted to the sable color of the German Shorthair and was supposed to have been destroyed at birth.

A month or so later a young officer came into my office and told me they were going to have to get rid of the dog because he was just too big for their apartment and his mother-in-law had told him if I wanted the dog it was mine. If not, he was to be sent back to New Orleans. Without a moment's hesitation, I accepted their offer and that very day I took Kelly back to our trailer park. There was a large fenced dog pen and dog house, which became his home until we were to return to Wisconsin. My first task was to teach him basic obedience to simple commands. I spent time working with him using a choke chain and a short leash. He was a very powerful animal and could drag Olive across the yard in her sixth month of pregnancy with her feet braced. The next lessons consisted of teaching him to retrieve. I made a smallish ball of barbed wire and covered it with a piece of cloth so when he picked it up he had to be careful. He learned the lesson well and when we got home to the farm he could catch chickens and bring them to you without pulling feathers.
I planned on using him for pheasant hunting, but as there were no pheasants in Georgia I trained him on wild quail at an old airport outside the city. He was never fast enough to hold the quail on a point; they would keep moving in front of him, and so he learned to keep moving forward slowly until the birds flushed. When we hunted pheasants he would do the same, so I learned that when he went to point I had better get ready to shoot, because he was going to keep going until the bird flushed. He had another very curious habit for which I had no explanation; he would point snakes, even snake's skins, so while we were down south you never knew what to expect. Fortunately this was never a problem in Wisconsin or South Dakota.

When I was discharged and ready to go home, there was the problem of getting two of them that to Wisconsin. I had acquired another eight week-old Weimaraner female puppy named Dixie from a grateful client, because I had saved their litter from a deadly hookworm infection. Fortunately the Base Chaplain, Father Jordan, was going home to Wisconsin and could take our car along with the dogs.

Section Three: Palmyra

Chapter 23

In October of 1958 Kelly and I made our first trip to South Dakota in pursuit of the famous landlocked salmon, along with Jim Omdoll, Dr. Nitardy, Woody Wilson, Art Schmidt, and Ambrose X Cummings with his dog Linda. We ended up on a dairy farm in the middle of the state with the Brandrups, Les and Fran. The hunting was fantastic with five birds as a daily limit and 25 the bag limit. In three days we shot over 150 pheasants.

The first day, we hunted a couple of cornfields with a swale, like a little marsh in between. We had chased a large number of birds into it and so that evening I took Kelly down in it and walked about one-half. He flushed 13 birds and I downed 12 and he retrieved 11, and by the time we left my hunting jacket was full. I had birds under my belt all the way around and both hands full. Ambrose had been hunting on the hillsides with Linda and had seen the entire performance. He told me "Dr. you will never forget this experience," and obviously he was very right.

We returned for the first week of this season with the fellows for several years. I had a enjoyed myself so much that I wanted to share the experience with Olive, and so for several years we went with Katy and Dick Beischel along with their dog Champ. We hunted along the railroad tracks and smaller areas of cover and we always got birds, which Kelly would point and flush and quickly retrieve. When a bird got up he would start immediately after it, confident it was going down. If you shot two birds at one time you never had to worry about the first bird.

One-year they had had a great deal of rain and some fields were filled with water to the top of the fence posts. We found that we could have a great deal of success if we drove the fields towards the water and the pheasants had to flush at the water's edge. I shot a rooster and it fell in the water beyond the fence. Kelly swam out, climbed the fence, retrieved the bird, dropped it on the other side, climbed over the fence again and brought the bird to me. He hated ducks and did not want to put them in his mouth because of their odor. One day we shot a duck in the middle of a dugout, which is a man-made pond to provide water for the cattle. I tried repeatedly to have him retrieved it and finally he picked it up by the bill and brought it to me. Another time we shot a couple of mallards out of the car window and sent him after them; he went directly to the spot but pretended there was nothing there. We finally had to go into the grass and pick them up. He always instinctively knew when we were leaving for South Dakota and he would whimper and pace his kennel until he was loaded in the back of the station wagon. It was over 600 miles to Brandrup's, and he would stand and whimper with his head over Olive's shoulder all the way until we turned of the main highway onto the gravel road in front of the farm and then he would get more excited with each passing minute until he was barking furiously.

I'm sorry that there is no happy ending to this tale, but one morning I found him dead in his kennel with a twisted stomach. I know he died a very painful death, but I also know I will always remember him as the first great dog I ever owned.

Chapter 24

Waldo and Irene Schearer were a middle-aged childless couple who lived on a small farm southwest of Eagle. Waldo had a deep gravelly voice which was easily recognizable. You never had to ask who was calling when he was on the phone. Irene worked for years and years as a telephone operator for the North West telephone company in town, and I used to stop at the office while I was delivering papers in the evening and visit her.

So it was only natural that when I set up practice, they were my clients. Waldo got his clothes caught in a piece of farm machinery and died some months later. At the time of my tale, Irene lived alone with her huge collie, Charlie, who this story is about. It was Good Friday afternoon when I received a call from the neighbor that Charlie had been hit by a car in front of their house. I knew there was no chance of Irene bringing him into the office, so I jumped in my truck and hurried out to pick him up.

Charlie was a huge dog nearly the size of a Saint Bernard and his skin had been torn on one side of his body from his shoulder back to his hip. There were no broken bones or massive bleeding, but he was in shock. My son Kevin was home from college, and he aided me in transporting him to the office and putting him on the examining table. I treated him for shock, and then anesthetized him because I could see this was going to take a lot of time. I sutured the skin as best I could, putting in nearly 100 sutures while Kevin assisted. There were some areas where were the skin had been torn so badly I knew it would not heal by first intention. I was also aware that if Irene saw him in this condition she would want to put him down, but I was sure I could save him.

I called and informed her what had happened, and that Charlie would have to be hospitalized for some time. He was so big that he would not fit comfortably in one of my cages, so he was laid on a blanket on the floor. As the days went by, I gradually removed the sutures slowly, taking out every other one; but as I had feared there was an area larger than the size of my hand that would have to granulate in, and so every day I would debride the area and dress it with antibiotic cream while Charlie lay on his side, never moving a muscle. This went on for nearly three weeks; all the while he roamed free in the office. Some clients received a great start when they opened the office door and were greeted by him. Finally, when the area was about the size of a silver dollar, I took him back home and Irene was more than delighted. I stopped at the farm a couple more times to treat the sore. She was concerned that he might bite me, but I told her we had been through a lot together.

One day, she lay down on the couch and died of a heart attack. Some of her nephews wanted me to euthanize Charlie, but I absolutely refused because he meant too much to me. I took him home and put him in the office once again. One night while on a call to farm couple near Helenville who were childless and in late middle-age, I noticed a large empty dog house by the back door and I inquired what had happened to their dog. They explained that he had been killed by a car, in front of the house, and they missed him deeply. Ironically, their names were Carl and Irene.

Suddenly a light came on in my head, and I told them I wanted to give them a present, but if they didn't want it, it had to come back to me. The very next day, I delivered Charlie and they were amazed. They sent me a letter saying it was the nicest thing anyone had ever done for them, but they told me he had one habit they couldn't explain. If anyone lay down on the sofa, he would whine and nuzzle them so they couldn't take a nap.

Chapter 25

Warren Arndorfer had called in the morning to check a cow that was off feed, but it was nearly noon when I arrived at the farm. It had not been a real good morning; I had to blood test an entire herd of cattle for a second time because the blood had frozen in the mail and hemolized, so it was gratis. While I was waiting for Warren to come down to the barn, I decided to check a bull that I had treated a couple of days earlier. I took his temperature, checked for rumen mobility and used a compass to make sure the magnet I had given him was in the right place. About that time I finished he appeared and apologized for not seeing me drive in because he had been eating lunch.

It was early February with not the slightest sign of spring, and the cattle were all in the barn. He pointed out an ordinary-looking Guernsey, who was lying in her stall and appeared normal in all respects. I attempted to get her up with a gentle nudge on her rear legs, but she refused to cooperate, and so I checked her temperature, which was normal. I wanted to see if her intestines were functioning, so I kicked her a little harder to make her stand, and with that she turned her head toward me, gave a little moan, and died. We both looked on in amazement.

I decided this was too much and I had to know what killed her, so I did a necropsy, which proved nothing. All of her thoracic and abdominal abdomenal contents were as normal as could be . I thought I had seen and unusual look in her eyes when she turned her head just before dying, and I decided to remove her head and take it to Madison to be checked for rabies. I was going to hand-deliver the blood samples to the state veterinary diagnostic lab because I didn't want to chance them being frozen again. I wore heavy rubber gloves while doing the post and I placed the head in a plastic garbage bag. I told the farmer to wear gloves when he cleaned up the manger and the drinking cups and disinfect with chlorine solution.

The next afternoon, the Warren's wife received a call from the state lab of hygiene stating the cow had been rabid, and she panicked. When you mention rabies, most people think of an animal frothing at the mouth and being extremely aggressive. However, there is another form called dumb rabies, and this was what had killed my patient. Warren had to undergo a series of shots because he thought I was blowing smoke when I suggested the possibility of rabies, and had not used any precautions when cleaning up. While I had been in in vet school, a large Holstein bull had been a patient, and two doctors and four students had been exposed to him before the diagnosis of dumb rabies. When I think back about my case, I realize God must have been looking over my shoulder that day. If I had gotten to the farm earlier, I would have probably treated her by giving milk of magnesia bolas from my mouth and been exposed to her saliva. She would have died, and the farmer thought, "Doc blew this one," and never bothered to tell me. I would have been exposed to rabies and never known it. When I talked to him later, he remembered there had been a skunk in the barnyard in October. It may take up to a year after exposure before an animal shows symptoms. I have had one other experience with rabies where the end result was not as good, but that is another tale.

Chapter 26

The people of North prairie and the town of Genesee considered Sol Engel to be the richest farmer in the county, and perhaps the state. He owned four dairy farms, a goat farm, a spring water bottling plant, and a supper club with a bowling alley. I found him to be a fascinating individual both as a client and a friend. He had the reputation of being an unscrupulous businessman, but I learned most of the time it was undeserved. Sol was a very vengeful individual, having worked hard for every cent he had, and he wasn't about to be cheated. Instead of "an eye for an eye" with him, it was "an eye for a head".

I remember on one occasion he asked me to pregnancy examine some cattle he had purchased, and when I told him all three of them were open, and I would write a statement stating so. He said, "Doctor, don't worry. They screwed me, but I will screw them back worse."

On another occasion he hired a couple of young men to whitewash three barns. The mixture of whitewash was too weak, and they soon needed to be redone. When he approached those fellows they only laughed at him, so the next year he had them white wash five barns and refused to pay them.

He was usually chauffeured in his Ford Thunderbird by one of his tenant farmers named Friske. I never heard him addressed by any other name than "Friske, you S O B", and one day he deserved the title. Sol had been to an auction and purchased three large Texas Longhorns, which they had to separate from the rest of the cattle because of their horns. I tried in vain to convince him to slaughter them and not bother to dehorn, and Friske derided me saying he wasn't afraid to do it. A couple of days later I took the cattle chute to the farm, and had finished with two of them when Sol and Friske showed up. I gave him a bad time about getting there when the job was nearly done. Friske took the saw and proceeded with the last steer, but unfortunately the animal fell down in the chute and strangled to death before I could release him. Sol screamed at the top of his voice, "Friske, you S O B, you did that on purpose, but you are not going to get any of that meat!"

Sol was a shrewd judge of cattle, and had made his money purchasing milking cows for a large dairy farm. He was paid a certain amount of money for each one that produced so much milk. He loved to attend farm auctions and pick up bargains. One time he purchased an entire herd of Jersey cattle because there were few buyers there.

As I say he always treated me fairly, and one time he told me, "Friske owes you money and you will never collect, but you are a young man with a family and need it, so I will pay you and deduct it from what I owe him. On several occasions when we had injured cattle, he would say, "Don't worry Doc, we'll send her to the club." Needless to say, when I ate at the club, I ordered fish.

Chapter 27

I have always had an affection for my large animal clients. These farmers and their families were a large part of my life, and I hope I was a small part of theirs. However the Lidicker brothers, Jack and Alvin, were exceptions. Jack had never married, and had attended St. John's Military Academy and Michigan State University. Alvin had been married, but his wife and family had left him years ago, and he should have attended reform school. He walked with a limp but that was not his only problem he suffered from ocular rectitis, a condition wherein the nerve to your eye becomes crossed with the nerve to your rectum and you have a shitty outlook on life. They lived in Palestine, with their ancient mother who couldn't sleep well at night, and so their entire day was five hours late. Many times they would call for service after 8:00 p.m., and I have delivered lambs and calves after midnight.

When I try to analyze my dislike for them, several reasons come to mind. First, they were lousy farmers, their barns were always dirty and dark. I enjoyed working for people who had pride of ownership, but there was none there. They were always about five months behind in their field work. I remember one day in particular, some farmers were preparing to plant corn while others were finishing sowing grain, but the Lidickers were threshing last year's shocks of grain covered with weeds.

I was always addressed as "Crawley," and spoken like calling the dog. No matter how much I went out of my way to help them, it was never appreciated. After their mother died, they moved to a farm outside of Little Prairie, and I would stop there to check the heifers in heat and breed them artificially. The beams in the barn were covered with empty beer bottles. So when Alvin called to tell me that his milk cows had been poisoned by drinking from the lake in which the D N R had put copper sulfate to control the algae, and he was going to sue the state for big money, I felt it was time to get revenge for all my misgivings and problems. I told him I would have to bring in a veterinarian from the state. I had had occasion to call upon Dr.Krohn, an egotistical individual who knew all the answers. No matter what the problem, it was a lack of good management by the owners. I could never take him back a second time to a farm or they would have killed him when he got out of the car. When I called him I said, "Don't come until after 10:30, as he will still be in the barn," and he replied, "Oh, one of those kind."

When we arrived, after a few minutes, Alvin and came out of the house carrying a sandwich, and loudly announced, "Okay you smart SOB's. You were in college while I had to stay home and work. What's wrong with my cows?"

I could see the chip on Krohn's shoulder grow to the size of a woodpile. We spent more than an hour examining his feed and forage and taking copious notes. At last, Krohn turned to him and said, "I know what's wrong with your cows. They bad are suffering from hollow gut, caused by empty mangers disease, and if you don't get some good feed into those animals in the next 24 hours, I will have the humane society here, and you will spend time in the county jail, and someone else will have these animals."

For once in his life, Alvin was speechless, and we turned and left the farm. Needless to say, I was never once called back, but it had been worth it.

Chapter 28

I always believed that God in his infinite goodness would give a hunter two or three good dogs during his lifetime. I had already had one. I didn't have great expectations for Jan.

Donnie Lean was a 40 year-old bachelor, and as odd as a $3 bill. After his father died, he lived all alone across the street from the Methodist Church in a large two-story house. After graduation from high school he had attended the University of Wisconsin Oshkosh and roomed with Squeak Wilson. He never left the dorm for the first two weeks and finally came home. He was an only child and never had a job in his life, as his dad stated "I have plenty of money for Donnie and me for life."

One cold and snowy day in December, he called to say, "You have to come and pick up my dog, because I can't take care of her."

I had treated the dog on occasion over the years. She was a small Brittany Spaniel, spayed and nicely marked. We had gotten a lot of snow already that year, and I pushed through it over my knees to a small pen and dog house in the backyard, and carried her back to my truck to bring her home. My youngest son, Patrick, was in grade school, and I told him, "This is your dog." He fed and watered the dogs that were kenneled in the garage.

In early March, Donnie called for the first time in nearly four months and asked, "Do you still have my dog? I want her back." I explained he would have to pay board for the time I kept her, but he was determined to to pick up the dog. As he led the dog up the street, he met Patrick coming home from school. With tears streaming down his face Patrick faced me and said, "Dad, that is my dog." I tried to explain it was really Donnie's, and that I had to give it back to him.

About two weeks later I received a call from the Jefferson County

John E. Crawley, DVM

Humane Society, inquiring about the inoculation status of a Brittany Spaniel carrying my tag. I lied when I told them it was my dog, and had been stolen. She had been found in Fort Atkinson by the police department and turned over to the Humane Society. I immediately went to Fort Atkinson, paid the fine, and picked her up at the Humane Society's kennels after paying her board bill. When I returned home I gave her to Pat and said, "No one will ever take her away from you again." It seemed that Donnie had given the dog to some people in Fort and she ran away.

When October rolled around, I headed for South Dakota for my annual migration, along with Jana (we had changed her name). I didn't know what to expect because the only birds she had ever hunted were woodcock, or cockadoodles, which are small migratory birds found around ponds. I was amazed and pleased by her reaction to pheasants. She performed as well as anything a bird hunter could imagine, and I knew God had given me my second good dog.

One year when pheasants were scarce, there had been lots of rain on the prairies, leaving areas of pond water that were covered with all sorts of ducks. I took Jana and waded up to my knees. I had shot only a couple (which she retrieved), before she started to watch the sky and whimper with excitement when duck appeared.

Patrick was in college, and had returned home for Thanksgiving. Jana was in her kennel, in bad shape with cancer. He said, "Dad, we can't let her be this way. We have to put her to sleep."

I told him, "Patrick, she is your dog, and I wanted you to make the decision."

Chapter 29

Bonnie Highland farm was the home of John and Elfrida Wilson and their four children, Kemp, Wiley, Trelyn and Welody. John was what I had always envisioned a Scotsman to be. He was tall with a ruddy complexion, and was never in a hurry nor excitable, even the time I reopened an umbilical abscess on a calf, and watched with horror as the intestines spilled out on to the ground from a hernia. He walked with a shuffle and had stooped shoulders. He always addressed me as "Doctor," although for over 45 years most people call me "Doc" (I hope with affection).

Elfrida was a woman of the 90's, but this was the 60's, and I always felt she was born 30 years ahead of time. She was very quick in action and awareness, and she believed in living life to the fullest. Her hair was cut in a boy's bob, she wore blue jeans and rubber boots, but was a lady in every sense of the word. She was interested and involved in a county and local politics, the school system, and especially her children. I believe she was much younger than her husband, and in her last years she would go to the barn daily to help Kemp with the milking and chores when John was no longer able to work. Unfortunately, they found her dead in bed after she failed to show up one morning at the barn. She had willed her body to the University of Wisconsin Medical School, and they picked her up that same morning. The family never had a memorial service or anything for closure. As one of the neighbors remarked, "It was like having a cow die and calling the rendering truck." I remember sitting at the kitchen table for coffee and rolls and looking at the family tree painted on the wall and across the ceiling.

Kemp was the oldest of the children and worked with his parents are around the farm. I don't recall ever seeing the other three in the barn. He belonged to the local 4-H Club and showed calves at the county fair. Although the Wilsons had some purebred Holsteins, the competition at the show was very stiff and he never did very well.

John E. Crawley, DVM

There was only one purebred Aryshire breeder in the county, so John decided if Kemp was ever to win a blue ribbon, Aryshires were the answer. So they went out and purchased some heifers. Now, John and Kemp were not going halfway, so they left the horns on, and they put weights and the pulley to train them, so they stood straight up. Those massive horns would measure 3 feet between the tips, and people marveled at them while he did very well at the shows. However, he left the farm to attend the University and John had to have a sale of the cows, as he was unable to care for them because of his age. Although people admired these animals with the outstanding horns, no one wanted to take them home and put them with their horn-less animals, and most of the cows ended up at the stockyards to be slaughtered.

John was a collector, mostly old farm machinery which was to be in his museum. Among the things he collected was a treadmill, which turned a shaft he had attached to a corn sheller. He trained a large male goat to walk on the treadmill, which he did very well. One day, John called to tell me that William the goat had fallen off the treadmill and broke his leg, and would I come and set it. When I got to the farm, I could see that his diagnosis was correct. The problem was I had no casting material with me, so and I went into town to the medical center to get some. They looked at me with a great deal of skepticism when I told them I needed to set a Billy goat's leg, but when I told them the animal belonged to John Wilson, the doctors smiled and nodded. The leg healed well, and in a month he was back on the treadmill, and John saved the cast to put in his museum. While I was working on the animal, John asked if I had ever seen a Billy goat that gave milk. I smiled at him, and thought, "you have been out in the sun too long." He got a small glass and started milking, and to my amazement, a milky solution flowed from the teats. I didn't taste it, but to all appearances it was milk. John theorized that when the goat was walking on the treadmill, his testicles had massaged the udder, and stimulated the production of milk.

Chapter 30

I first met Stan Leverenz when he called to have me to examine a problem breeder. He had a small herd of Guernsey cattle just outside of North Prairie. He had repeatedly bred this animal but could not get her in calf. After checking her, I decided they were inseminating her before she had ovulated so he said, "As long as you are here, go ahead and breed her." When I first started my practice, I decided a good way to meet dairy farmers was to do artificial insemination, so I bred cattle for Curtis Candy Farms. You got paid for the first service and anything after that was free to the owners. I ended up servicing lots of problem breeders around the county. I think I was at Stan's seven times every 21 days before I got that animal pregnant. When she delivered, the calf had a bulldog face and was a monster. He gently chided me that after all that time I should have at least gotten a complete calf. The winked at me and said, "let's have some fun." He had called the local livestock dealer to send a cow out to the stockyards, and when Eddy Mueller showed up, he told him he had a very nice Guernsey calf that he did not want to raise because it was summer, and he would give it to him free. Eddy was all smiles until we got to the calf pen and he saw the calf and the expression on his face changed to horror. "Oh Stan, I could never take that animal!" he protested, but Stan kept insisting until Eddy nearly ran from the barn.

The Golden Guernsey Dairy tried to encourage their patrons to upgrade to purebred animals, and every year they would hold a consignment sale at which purebred breeders' would send some cows. Unfortunately, most of these animals had a hole in them and the farmers that bought them got stuck. Stan had purchased such an animal a couple of years earlier that had been consigned by one of the noted purebred breeders in Waukesha County. He took her home and when she freshened she gave a great deal of milk, but after he turned the herd out to pasture, her production dropped drastically. He couldn't figure out what had happened until one day he caught her sucking her own udder. Stan figured that you had to find your jackknife where you lost it, so the next spring he sent the cow back to the consignment sale. The previous owners looked at her but never said a word. After the sale was over, Curt Orchard, a very tight fisted individual approached Stan to say "I bought your cow" and Stan told him "She is one of the best milkers I have in the herd." A couple of months later Curt was pounding on the door saying, "Stan, you have to take that cow back because she sucks herself." Stan merely smiled and said, "I told you she was one of the best milkers in the herd."

Chapter 31

Hollywood is not all it's cracked up to be. Los Angeles is full of fruits, nuts, and traffic jams, but if we had won $24,000, I probably would have a different opinion. Our family had always maintained we would be great on Family Feud, so when Ellen learned they were going to hold auditions in Madison, it was all we needed. We decided the team would consist of the four oldest children and me. Kevin declined in favor of his wife, D.P. (Diana Paulina). We all showed up in Madison on a Monday morning. We were interviewed and played the game before a lovely middle aged lady, who treated us with kid gloves and told us how wonderful we where. However, if we didn't hear from them by Thursday, we would never hear from them again.

Over 1200 families from southern Wisconsin were interviewed in the next three days. We received the call on Wednesday to be back Friday to meet the producer of the show, Mr.Felcher. D.P. lived in Iowa City, Kathleen was a radio newscaster in Dixon, Illinois, Ellen was a law student in Madison and Sara worked as a waitress and bartender in Milwaukee. I explained the problem of getting them all together again and could we substitute one of the other family members, but they insisted it had to be the same people. We finally agreed we would be the first family interviewed Friday evening.

The producer proved to be exactly the opposite of our first contact. He ridiculed me for my haircut, gave Kathleen a bad time about being a journalist, and tried to set up a date with Sara. I was completely convinced he was a California idiot, and I didn't care if we ever got on the show. Kevin explained he was just trying to see how we would react if Richard got testy. I read in the paper later they had called back 64 families and selected 12 to go to Hollywood.

We received a letter inviting us to be on the show on November 11th. They provided five airline tickets, a station wagon, and three hotel rooms on Hollywood Boulevard for four days along with $500 for

John E. Crawley, DVM

spending money. I ordered five more airline tickets and another station wagon so that the entire family could go. When we arrived at the hotel, I was told to call the TV station immediately. I was told that Richard was sick and there would be no filming that week. I told them I had brought the entire family and we were not going right home. They said the arrangements were the same and we could stay. We spent the next five days visiting Universal Studios, Knott's Berry Farm, and the racetrack and partying.

A year from the following April we got word to return. The fellows in the poker club had suggested I take a gift to Richard emblematic of my profession, so I acquired a cane made from the "best part" of a bull. My daughters were embarrassed, and made me promise not to tell anyone what it was. The studio insisted I not mention it on the air, so when I gave it to him I called it a genuine Wisconsin walking stick.

The TV studio was large barn like structure with bleachers. We were segregated upstairs in a ready room along with five other families. They taped five shows, one right after another, with a seven-minute pause. We were to bring several changes of clothing so it would appear to be different days. We were not to make any phone calls or contact other people until we were done taping. We were the fourth family called, and we played against a young man, his wife, her sister and his two sisters; and they had won over $20,000 already. Between shows, a high-school boy presented Richard with a painter's cap from their band. When Richard gave it to our opponent to wear the fellow wouldn't do it and I could see Richard was getting annoyed.

We were doing very well on the first two questions, but then we faltered and lost the next two. It came down to stealing the last answer of "What is the first thing you do when reporting for work." We guessed "read the paper", but the answer was "hang up your coat." We received some merchandise prizes, a small amount of money, and "Thanks for coming." Our opponents were ready to play for the fifth game when Richard asked, "How much money have you won?" The fellow replied "Over $24,000" and Richard remarked, "..and this is the third day you have worn the same sport coat!" showing his displeasure about the painter's cap.

The show was finally broadcast in June, and by that time all the people in Palmyra and Eagle were aware that Doc and his family were to be on TV. A salesman and his wife from Milwaukee who knew Sara stopped in Eagle at a tavern to watch the show and were amazed that the place was crowded with excited and cheering people. He didn't know it was my hometown.

Chapter 32

Once upon a time, south of Dousman, along Highway D, there lived three farmers; rather there was only one farmer and two noblemen residing on the same farm. Eugene Menge was the farmer and the two noblemen were his brothers-in-law, Steve Lewandowski and Ralph Laning. They were actually brothers, although their appearance was completely opposite. Ralph and Eugene were both large men, well over 6 ft. tall and weighing nearly 250 pounds each, while Steve stood about 5 ft. 7 and weighed 135 soaking wet. Eugene was a graduate engineer and had worked in Alaska on the oil pipeline. He was a jolly fellow, always pleasant, with a perpetual smile on his face. He never seemed to rebel against the constant "supervision" rendered by the other two. They were both lawyers, but where and when they had ever practiced, I could not say. They each lived in one of the three houses on the farm. Steve had never married and lived alone, Eugene and their sister had no children and lived next door, while Ralph, his wife and two daughters lived alongside. During the time that I knew them, Steve became a math teacher at Whitewater University and was there for several years. Ralph had a full time job telling Eugene what to do and how to do it.

They had started to build a new barn years before I knew them, and it was still unfinished 20 years later. They were not really good farmers, and I could not figure out where their money came from, but they had several real estate holdings in Milwaukee and played the stock market, buying and selling a block of stock at a time.

Ralph just loved to see me come so he could pick an argument with me. No matter what the subject, he would ask my opinion, and then proceed to argue against it while I was treating the cattle. It took me some time to realize what was happening. When I caught on, I would /take the opposite stand of what I had said previously, and watch him reverse himself. All the while Steve and Eugene would listen in great delight to the discussion, as they wouldn't argue with Ralph.

This game between us continued for many years, until they decided to quit milking and sell the cows. I have often thought of them and marveled that the three of them got a long, considering the differences in their personalities.

Chapter 33

What do you do or say when you go into a barn and find the farmer screaming and cursing obscenities at the top of his voice, kicking the tires and pounding on the hood of his tractor with a crank. His face was bright red, with tears running down his cheeks, and the veins in his neck bulging. I had never seen an individual so out of control and frustrated with an inanimate object. I nearly turned and beat a hasty retreat out of there, but instead I quietly said, "Bud, can I help you?" It seemed that he had recently overhauled the tractor, and now it was parked, with the manure spreader, in the middle of the barn and would not start. He had tried and tried until now the battery was dead and he had been cranking if by hand. I suggested that we bring in his other tractor and pull it out of the way. I breathed a silent prayer, "Please, God let this one start."

I knew from past experience that Bud Bergland had a bad temper, because I had treated a cow with pitchfork marks from her heels to her hips. That temper would prove to be the ruination of him. Sometime later that very cow had her revenge. Bud was walking out of milking her with a full pail of milk when she kicked him and broke both bones in his leg. He went to the doctor's office to have it set, and they placed it in a plaster cast from his hip to his heel. When they removed the cast six weeks later, the fracture was not healed and the bottom of his heel had ulcerated because of pressure necrosis. He went to the hospital in Madison and had steel pins inserted in the bones. To attempt a skin graft to repair the heel they forced it up to his thigh with a cast for a month. The cramps and pain was so unbearable that he suffered a nervous breakdown while in the hospital. After about 18 months he was able to go back to farming and milking cows. He told me he was going to sue the doctor for malpractice and would collect enough money that he would never have to work again. I tried to convince him to talk to the doctor first, but he would have no part of that .He was going to "fix that S.OB. good."

When you start to sue for big money the insurance companies bring out their big guns and such was the case this time. They presented all of his tax papers for the previous five years to show he had not made much money, so loss of income was not a factor. They brought in witnesses to testify as to his character and behavior in front of a jury. He was ridiculed and showed to be a troublemaker, and in the end the jury awarded him nothing. However, the judge ruled he should receive some damages, but not nearly what he had been asking. He was a very bitter man, his wife and children left him, and he lost the farm when the bank foreclosed on his mortgage.

John E. Crawley, DVM

Chapter 34

I have always considered raising dairy calves an art form. The ability to give those little fellows just the right amount of milk to keep them growing at the fastest possible rate and not give them an ounce too much (that would cause a gastric upset) was a gift. If the milk got into the first stomach, the rumen, it would ferment and cause diarrhea and the calf would stop eating.

In all of the years that I worked for Lucian Marsh, I never once had to treat a calf with scours. He was far and away the best at raising calves of anyone I have ever met. Lucian and Helen raised three fine sons who helped in the barn, but he never let anyone feed the calves but him. From the first time I was called to the farm, I was always treated like a son, and my wife often remarked if they had a daughter I would never have married her. Lucian would give each of the sons a calf each year, but it had to be a bull calf because he said if they got heifer calves soon they would own half of the herd and the milk check.

One year when I was artificially breeding the cows, he decided to breed the young stock to beef bulls because he didn't usually save the female calves from them, and use dairy bulls on the older cows. It seemed like a good idea, but you don't give ahead of Mother Nature. The beef calves were females while the dairy calves were mostly bulls. Lucian was scrupulously honest. He sent milking cows to the stockyards that he could have sold to other farmers but he said, "if they are not good enough for me they shouldn't be good enough for someone else."

The oldest son Dale got married first, and later had a herd of purebred Polled Herford cattle while he ran a milk route for Golden Guernsey dairy. He delivered our milk for many years. Philip and Tom were home on the farm for the first 10 to 15 years I worked for the Marsh's. They were both great fellows, and in all the time I spent with them and their father, I never heard a cross word between them, which was not the case in lots of other families. They were both good students in high school, and exceptional athletes. They lettered in basketball and football all four years. Phil married a pretty young girl from Whitewater named Carmen and years later they lived in our upstairs flat. Phil continued to work with his father until they sold the farm to the Godfrey company.

Tom's story didn't turn out quite so well. After graduating from high school, he started college at the University of Wisconsin Whitewater and was doing very well. Coming home one winter evening, he skidded on some ice and smashed into a stone wall. He was hospitalized for quite some time and suffered permanent brain damage. As they say, he was never quite right after that and the saddest part he knows it. He tried to go back to college, but he just could not make it go. He later married a girl from town and raised a couple of fine sons while working at the dairy plant in Waukesha.

While Lucian and Helen were still on the farm, he developed throat cancer and had his larynx removed so he could only talk in a whisper as he refused to use the artificial one. I considered it a great honor and privilege to serve as a pall bearer when he died.

Chapter 35

Our daughter, Colleen Jean, was in second grade when Lady Dixie of Lynwood joined our family. She was a beautiful Shetland Collie puppy which I had delivered, along with her litter mates, on New Year's Eve at the home of Reverend Chase Paige. How a little girl with three sisters and two brothers could be lonely I will never know, but I was told she was, and needed a dog of her own, and hence Dixie.

They got along famously and Colleen would share all of her troubles and joys with her in their bedroom. Unfortunately, one day in the fall, when the family was in the yard raking leaves, they forgot to bring her into the house and she was hit by a car and killed.

The Paiges had kept another puppy that was to be a show dog. He was perfect in every way, except that the tips of his ears did not bend over. When they learned that Dixie had been killed, the father told his young daughter, Paige, that she should give either the mother or the puppy to us. I thought it was a very tough decision for a young girl to have to make, but Bonnie Prince Charlie filled a large void in our daughter's life.

I will never know why he did not like me. He would never come to me or let me pet him as long as he lived. Whenever I came home and got out of my truck he would circle me, barking furiously. However, when anyone else came, including strangers he would run out to greet them, wagging his tail. He would not come into the house for me unless I held the door open and turned my back. If we were alone at night with a severe thunderstorm he might come over to my chair, but only then. He suffered a series of mishaps during his lifetime. He swallowed a needle and thread, which lodged in his throat that I operated on to remove. He was hit by cars three times; once breaking a leg, which I set and cast, he had a bad concussion which left him deaf in one ear, and nearly died a third time from shock. After each of these occasions, he would be my friend for about a week, and then it was back to the same old behavior. I told him he was the most ungrateful dog I had ever known, as I had helped him heal four times and that was the way he thanked me.

When Colleen left home to go to college in Madison, she wanted to take Charlie. We had purchased a duplex so that the kids would have a decent place to live while attending school. She lived the first year in a dorm, but as soon as she moved into the house she took her dog. One Saturday afternoon after a football game, I was seated in their living room when Charlie came over and sat by my chair. I remarked to the girls that Charlie must be sick, and asked how he had been acting. Colleen told me that he had slowed down a great deal and she had to carry him home from one of their walks. When I examined him I discovered that one of his testicles was very swollen and painful to the touch. I told her that I would take him home and try to treat him. I gave him hormones antibiotics and painkillers, but he did not improve and grew weaker with each passing day. I vowed I would not go to extraordinary means to save, him but I ended up with intravenous feedings and medication. One day Dennis built casket for Charlie, and he died that evening.

I removed the swollen testicle and submitted it to the state diagnostic lab for analysis. Nearly three months passed before I received a report that they had never seen such a specimen, and had to refer it to the medical school. It seems that Charlie had a fetal twin, which started to grow after 12 years, which killed him. They wished that I had sent them fixed tissue instead of frozen, so they could have published the results in a National Research Journal.

Chapter 36

On March 18, 2004, the world crashed for the Pett family. Warren and Donna were murdered by insurgents, at the school where they taught as agricultural missionaries, in Drenzai, Uganda. They were shot to death as they left their burning hut, leaving behind in Wisconsin three teenaged children, Solomon, Maurita and Ezra. They had been in Uganda for a little over a year after serving four years in Nairobi, Kenya.

The Pett family had been clients and friends for over 30 years. Norman and Irene had settled on the home farm to raise their children, Warren and Eileen, and milk Holsteins for the Golden Guernsey dairy. Irene had gone to school with my father years before. I made monthly visits to their farm to do pregnancy examinations, calf-hood vaccinations, and other routine veterinary duties. Theirs was the first herd I diagnosed with John's disease and set up a vaccination program. I always enjoyed my visits to the Pett's as they treated me like one of the family. When Warren and Donna were married, they moved into the old farmhouse while the old folks moved into a new one across the road. They continued to run the farm together, but Warren and his family did most of the work of dairying.

After about 12 years, Warren received a calling to become a missionary in Africa. He and Donna had an auction and sold the farm machinery and cattle. They pulled up stakes, and along with the youngest child, they headed for Kenya. They came back for a couple of months before returning to Africa alone. After their death, the church withdrew all of their missionaries from Uganda because they thought it was unsafe. The consolation for the family was that they had died as martyrs for God. The children are all now married, and one of them still lives in the old farmhouse, though the land has been subdivided and now raises homes instead of hay.

Chapter 37

Some days it doesn't pay to get out of bed, and I had such a day in February of 1974. We were having a blizzard, with winds about 30 miles an hour, and snow blowing in from the north. It was the kind of day that Wisconsin is famous for, and I hoped that the phone would not ring that day, but unfortunately, it started out about 7:30 a.m.

The farmer had young heifer, which he had been trying to get settled, pregnant, and had been unsuccessful. This morning she was in heat, meaning she would ovulate in the next few hours. She had to be inseminated within the next four to six hours, or we would have to wait 21 days, until she was fertile again. I tried to persuade him to wait because of the weather, but he pleaded would I please come and breed her that morning. He lived about 25 miles from Palmyra, and it was nearly 10:30 before I returned home.

I had no sooner gotten out of my insulated coveralls and boots when the phone started ringing again. This time it was a very excited woman from Paradise Springs, a resort outside of Eagle, who had a horse down in the snow. She told me that her regular veterinarian couldn't get there because of the weather and she needed help badly. I have often remarked, "I don't like horses and I don't care for the people that own them, for many reasons." The buildings were about half a mile uphill from the road. I was driving a Volkswagen truck, which would go through snow up over the bumpers. I had just started treating the prostrate animal when Dr. Howard Cook arrived on the scene. He had to leave his car at the gate because of all the snow, so any drugs we needed to use all came from me. He instructed me to give the animal cortisone, a large shot of vitamin B complex, a bottle of protein, I V, and another bottle of glucose, intravenous. Then he asked the woman owner if she had a bottle of wine, which she did because they ran a tavern. While she was gone to get it, I told Howard we should drink the wine and rub the empty bottle on the horse, then at least we would feel better, but he insisted we drench the animal with the wine. It was after 4:00 pm before I returned home again and it was still snowing and blowing, and I figured there was no way I could go out again.

We were eating supper when Bill Zettlemeir called to tell me that he had a cow that had cast her withers, a uterine prolapse, which is a very serious condition, and the animal would probably be dead by morning if it was not taken care of. He told me one of the roads was completely blocked, but I might be able to get through on another one, and he would come with the tractor to get me to the farm. After fighting the snow banks for another hour, I reached his barn only to find the animal was "cleaning," expelling her placenta, and my trip was totally unnecessary, and a waste of time and effort.

Three weeks later, the heifer I had bred came back into season and I had to rebreed her and so that had been a wasted call.

We got the horse onto a rug and dragged it back into the stable, but that night it got up, fell out of the door, and froze to death. Dr. Cook had gotten paid on the spot, but I had to wait over three months to collect. I told him that the next time I had to kill a horse, I could do it without his help.

Chapter 38

We were enjoying a Friday night fish fry at a tavern in Rome when the fellow seated at the next table remarked to his dinner companions, "Did you hear that damn fool young vet killed Bill Fryes bull?" This is not the kind of dinner conversation you like to hear, especially if you are that "damn fool young vet." I had been dehorning an18 month old bull when he collapsed and strangled himself about a week before, and evidently the word was out.

Bill and Clara Frye lived on a small rented farm north of town on Island Road. They were both in their late sixties but in good health. His facial appearance always reminded me of Mr. Peanut on Planters Peanuts cans. They were of slight of build and very active. They were great dancers and usually the last to leave the dance floor at any of the local dances. It was said that Bill could dance all night. They had been friends of my grandparents, who died in the 1940's, when they lived in Eagle and played cards together. The Fryes never had much money, but I always admired his optimism. He was always smiling, the crops were doing better, and the new heifers were milking just fine.
The only time I saw him down in the mouth was after Clara had a stroke and he was greatly worried about her. Fortunately she recovered with no ill after effects, and Bill was smiling again. At the time that the bull died I was doing artificial insemination, so I promised him that I would breed all of his cows free that year. We remained on friendly terms and I did all of his veterinary work until the day he retired and died. I always considered them to be friends of mine and I guess it was proved when I acted as a pallbearer for his funeral.

That was not the only bull I killed while dehorning. One Saturday morning, Cap Shindler had a large one that needed my attention, so I took my brother, Jerry, who was a university student with me to help. Cap was an old man and wouldn't be much help. We pulled the bull's head through a hole in the box stall and I started to saw. He promptly flipped himself over the boards and broke his neck. Jerry and I tried to revive him but Cap kept shaking his head saying, "The bull is dead boys, the bull is dead." We could not leave him in this situation, so we spent the next few hours butchering the animal. Cap was a good Swiss wine maker and very proud of his products, so after we had carried the meat into the house, we all sat down and enjoyed more than a couple of glasses of his homemade wine, and it tasted really good.

Chapter 39

"A friend is someone you know bad things about but you'd like them anyway" This is one of the axioms I learned from Ambrose A X Cummings, and another was, "Any man that says he is boss at home will lie about other things too." Ambrose and his wife lived on a small farm at the edge of town and raised purebred sheep. At one time his wife must have had red hair because he called her "Pinkie" and so did I, although her name was Dorothy. I guess he fully qualified as a friend because everyone knew in his younger days he had been a common drunk, even to the point of spending the night in the gutter on Main Street in Palmyra . He had committed himself to the state mental hospital and had taken the cure. He told me that when he was released he didn't know whether his wife would be there or not. They had a daughter named Mary but the next two children Kay and Mike didn't arrive until 14 years later.

He completely turned his life around and became a very successful businessman. He sold real estate and insurance, owned three farms, was active in the church, and was on the board of directors of the local bank. He was a well-known character in the village and led every parade on his Palomino mare, Goldie, wearing a big Stetson hat. There were people in town that didn't care for him, but I always felt they were merely jealous of his success. My father always told me to beware when dealing with him, but Dad warned me about a lot of people, until I finally told him that life was too short to be constantly worrying about being cheated.

In fact, Ambrose did me a huge favor, which I never for got. There was a lovely stone house with a seven-truck garage, which I fell in love with the first time I came to town. It had been built in 1941 by a contractor named Hayden Krause, who had moved to Arizona for his daughter's health. Ambrose had once sold the property to a trucker from town, but at the last minute Hayden backed out on the deal and made Ambrose look bad. Now Hayden was trying to borrow money

John E. Crawley, DVM

from the bank and Ambrose told me it was time to make a deal. He called Hayden and told him he thought he had a buyer but this time the price was final. When we settled, Ambrose gave me the real estate commission because, he said, I was a young man with a family. We have made this our home for the past 47 years, although the garage burned on June 9, 2004.

I spent a lot of good times with Ambrose hunting pheasants in South Dakota. He was a severe diabetic, but any time he wanted an extra piece of pie he just gave himself another shot of insulin. He was a terrible driver, and any time we went someplace I would try to get behind the wheel as soon as possible. He loved to play cards, and had a great Irish sense of humor. The only problem I had with him was that he was a staunch Democrat. I had the honor and the privilege of helping to carry him to his grave.

Chapter 40

Andrew John was nearly two and a half years old when I decided he needed a puppy. I had a client who bred and raised different breeds of dogs. At one time I vaccinated 23 for rabies at her home. She had a couple of black standard bred poodles which she had bred and when the first one whelped, she got the bitches confused and put the pups with the wrong dog, who immediately killed one and bit part of the ear off another.

I tried to suture it back in place but it would not heal. I named the poor little fellow Vincent Cantsew, and offered to buy him for my grandson. His dad was not too keen on the idea because he thought that poodles were sissy dogs until he saw the parents. Vincent proved to be somewhat of a nuisance in the household. There was a five month-old baby sister, and he developed a taste for disposable diapers and pacifiers. He would devour them every chance he got. He was kept in a large cage in the house while the parents both worked, and when they came home and let him out he would invariably urinate all over the carpet. After about a year and a half my daughter decided she could not put up with him any longer, and she told her mother that he had to go.

Our son Dennis was single and living alone in Portland, Maine where he worked in the theater, and when the opportunity came to adopt Vincent he jumped at the chance. They were constant companions and roommates for the next 10 years. They lived alone in Portland, Columbus, Ohio and Denver until his brother Pat moved to Denver also. Dennis had spent lots of hours training Vincent, and he knew a great many commands. If Vincent didn't respond immediately, Dennis would merely clear his throat to get results.

We were visiting the boys in Denver when Dennis came knocking on the door early Sunday morning. Vincent was bloated and I knew immediately he had a gastric torsion and needed help immediately.

His stomach had twisted on the long axis and shut off the blood supply. We found an emergency veterinary clinic, and I introduced myself to the young veterinarian and gave her my diagnosis. She asked if I would like to assist, and we immediately set to work. We tried to pass a stomach tube to relieve the gas but to no avail. Surgery was the only answer for Vincent, and he was over eight years old by this time. We corrected the torsion and sutured the stomach to the abdominal wall to hold it in place. The doctor gave me a professional courtesy and charged about half the normal fee. His recovery was uneventful at the time, but unfortunately Vincent would have recurring occasions of torsion and would have to be treated again and again. He was there so often he became a favorite of the staff, and Dennis would help in the clinic and receive no charges, except for drugs used.

We were all in New York for Pat's wedding when he got a call from Denver that Vincent had died. Dennis asked that he be placed in a freezer until he could return for a proper burial. He made arrangements with a friend to build a casket and with a bottle of Irish whiskey they would have a proper funeral for his old friend. The hole was already dug in the backyard and the friends gathered. When they opened the cadaver bag it was a different black dog. It was too late to cry, so they drank a toast and called it a day.

Chapter 41

The Jericho Creek runs through the middle of the Hickory Grove farm, which is my ancestral home. It was there that my great grandfather settled when he first came from Scotland in the 18 hundreds, and the birthplace of my maternal grandmother. He was of noble birth, but was disinherited when he married the stable keepers daughter, so became a ship's doctor.

The dairy farm was owned by George Rait when I became their veterinarian, and run by his two teenage sons, and a hired man and his family. George worked for Allis Chalmers in West Allis and drove there every day. His wife was completely crippled with rheumatoid arthritis and her body was twisted and shriveled. She had to be completely cared for, as she could not move to help herself. I was amazed and impressed by her four teenage children; Ruth, Dorothy, Robert and James, who showed all the love in the world in giving her care. Sometime later, they had an auction, sold the cattle and moved away, and I completely lost track of them. A number of years later they found a man's body along the creek, which the authorities believed had been there for over a year. It proved to be George, who had left a nursing home up north and returned to the old farm to die.

The next owner was a rich industrialist by the name of Thieme, who owned foundries all over the world. He completely remodeled the barn, put in stalls of oak, which he imported from Tennessee. Each one had a brass light fixture with a rheostat, a horse shower room; and money seemed no object. He hired an African American saddle bred horse trainer by the name of Joe Potter, who had forgotten more about training horses than most trainers ever knew. Joe always treated my brother and me with the greatest respect. I did not like horses or most of the people that own them, so the bulk of the horse work fell on Jerry. One day he told me that he was very uneasy treating $50,000 horses, and we should get a vet who was more qualified than us, or quit working for Mr. Thieme. This was the reason we formed the corporation with Dr. John Phelps.

I did have a couple of interesting experiences with Joe and the Tennessee Walkers. I was on call on Labor Day when he phoned to tell me they had a big problem. When I arrived, I found five dead mares, with their aborted fetuses behind them, in the pasture under a tree. It did not take me long to see they had been struck by lightning and electrocuted. I examined the rest of the horses to see if they had suffered any damage. About this time, Mr. Thieme arrived, and I inquired how much insurance he had on each of them, before I appraised them. He shook his head and said, "I don't think I ever purchased any." I thought to myself, "Better he had a $25,000 loss then one of my farmers."

Another interesting situation occurred when Joe called one day to inform me that Mr. Thieme had a horse that he wanted destroyed. I told him, "That is no problem. Just shoot the horse", but Joe insisted, "Mr.Thieme doesn't want me to shoot it." I said, "Just call the rendering company, and they will shoot it and haul the horse away." "No Doctor, Mr. Thieme wants to have you put the horse to sleep and bury him here on the of farm." It seemed that the animal had reared up and fallen over back word on his head. He had suffered permanent brain damage and was unpredictable in his behavior. The farm had several workers from the South, and one of them later described the situation like this. "It just looked like Martin Luther King's funeral. First came Joe leading the horse, then the doctor in his truck, Bill and Mike in the pick up, and then Frank with the tractor and the back hoe." They had hired a local construction company to dig a hole about the size of a small basement. Joe and I led the horse down into it, where I injected a barbiturate in to the jugular vein until the horse died.

A couple of years later, Joe called to ask some questions about breeding beef cattle. The accountant had told Mr. Thieme that he was going to have to show some profit from the farm if he was going to write it off as a tax deduction. I felt sorry for Joe, as he knew nothing about cattle, and suggested he find another position as a horse trainer, but he explained that Mr. Thieme had been very good to him, and he couldn't leave him now. That lasted about a year or so, and then the entire operation was sold.

Chapter 42

Dr. John Phelps was a sole practitioner in the neighboring village of Sullivan. He had graduated from Cornell University in the early 1950's and set up a veterinary practice. He and his wife Lois had four children who were born and raised there. The oldest was a daughter that I never knew very well, but John, Kim and Pam were all teenagers when we formed our corporation.

In a partnership each partner is liable for the debts of the others, both business and private, so we incorporated to escape that liability. Jerry and I had called our practice Tri- County Veterinary Services, so now we just added "Inc". We did not know him very well personally, but he had a great reputation as a horse practitioner, so he was just the kind of man we were looking for. We approached him with our proposition and he accepted.

I had known that his clients were very loyal to him. I would get calls from his area when he was away, but as soon as he returned they would not call me again, and I took this as a sign that he was a good veterinarian. He was good-hearted to a fault, but a poor businessman, and one of the most disorganized people I have ever met. He told us that he only sent out bills once or twice a year. We insisted that it had to change. He usually started out on his farm calls after 10:00 a.m., and didn't finish until after 8:30 in the evening. His farmers were used to this kind of service, but if we were going to work together this had to change. Jerry and I both had young families and we wanted to spend as much time as possible with them. Within six weeks after we started, together a horse fell on him, breaking both bones in his leg, and putting him a cast for five months. Since I was the closest to Sullivan, I inherited the bulk of his practice, and worked many long continuous days and nights. I got my first day off when my youngest son was born on August 1, 1970.

To illustrate my remark about being disorganized: John and Lois were going to take a week's vacation in New York to visit her mother. Several days later when I drove past their home I could see they had not left, so I stopped to see if they had trouble and they told me they could not find the car keys.

John had been doing his small animal practice in the basement of their home, and we soon decided this was not going to work, so we purchased a retired doctor's home and office. We hired a local woman to answer the phone and dispatch the calls over our mobile radios. When John had the radio in his home, frequently his youngest daughter would call to say she had missed the bus and needed a ride to a high school in Jefferson. We got very used to hearing her pleading, "But Daddy, but Daddy!" sometimes three or four times before he acquiesced.

The first veterinarian we hired was Dr. Gary Mirtz, who had graduated from Auburn University three years earlier. I had met him in Savannah, Georgia when I returned with the Air Force Reserve, and he was the post veterinarian. I convinced him to come to Sullivan when he was discharged. There was only one problem; his wife, Betty came from a small town in southern Louisiana. They were so far south that people from New Orleans were considered Yankees. That winter was one of the worst for snow and cold in over ten years. Betty went into hibernation in October, and didn't come out until the end of May. Needless to say, they both left at the end of summer and returned to Louisiana, where he practices to this day.

John E. Crawley, DVM

Chapter 43

To understand and appreciate this tale, you must know something about the digestive system of cattle. They have four stomachs; the first is called the rumen, the second is the reticulum, the third is the omasum, and the last is the abomasum. It is sometimes called the true stomach where the digestive enzymes are produced. The rumen is a very large organ and can hold up to 80 gallons. In it, fermentation occurs to break down the fiber in the diet. The cow regurgitates food to form a cud, chews it thoroughly, and swallows it again. The reticulum lies below and along side, and is the lowest part of the digestive system. Hence any metal or stones the cow might swallow will end up here, and because the entrance and exit are both higher it cannot get out.

Loose wires could pierce the stomach wall and cause a lot of trouble, resulting in hardware disease. That is the reason if you suspect they have hardware you pass a magnet by mouth, and it attracts the metal and stays there for the life of the cow. The omasum is a large organ filled with leaves of rough tissue much like pages in a book where the food is the ground to a liquid consistency. The abomasum sometimes will fill with gas that becomes trapped behind the rumen, and causes a condition known as abomasal torsion or displaced abomasum. When this happens the digestive system slows down and the animal goes off feed.

Such was the case when Gilbert Went called one Thursday, concerned about one of his Brown Swiss cows. When I examined her, I could hear the characteristic "ping" of gas trapped over fluids on her left side. I informed him of the diagnosis of displaced abomasum. He had two choices: either operate and replace the abomasum to its proper position and suture it there, or send the cow to the stockyards, as she would never get better. He decided to ship her rather than operate because she was not that good of a producer. You do not want to yard cows on Fridays because the meatpackers are not interested in holding them until Monday, so Gilbert was going to keep her in the barn until Monday.

Several weeks later when I was called to the farm to treat some calves he said, "As long as you are here Doc, I want you to check another cow." Brown Swiss cattle look pretty much alike, and I did not recognize the animal. After I had examined her thoroughly I told him I could find nothing wrong. He gave me a big grin and said, "This is the cow you told me would never get better." I asked him what had happened, and he explained he had gotten tired of keeping her in the barn, so on Sunday he let her out in the pasture, and she went to the farthest point up on a hill. When it became time to bring them in she refused to come, so he sent the farm dog after her. The dog chased her as fast as she could run down the hill and into the barn. When she reached her stall she fell and collapsed, and he was afraid she would die. He went to the house for supper, and when he returned to the barn, she was standing and eating and she hadn't stopped since. Obviously the abomasum had returned to its normal position because of the running.

Chapter 44

Dixie has always been one of my favorite names for a female dog. The first one was a registered Weimeraner puppy I received from a grateful client in Savannah Georgia, and so I thought it appropriate to call her Dixie. I had treated a litter of puppies that were infected with hookworms, which are a very dangerous parasite especially for puppies and are capable of killing them. Most intestinal parasites merely live on the food that the host has eaten, but hookworms burrow in to the walls of the intestines like tiny hypodermic needles and the blood flows thru them constantly so the host becomes very anemic. I had been successful in saving these puppies lives and the owners wanted me to have one of them. I told them it was not necessary but they insisted that I take one. I finally agreed and selected a female that had an umbilical hernia that would require surgery at some future date.

Father Jordan brought her and Kelly back to Wisconsin when I left the Air Force in 1957. They were staying at the farm in Little Prairie while we were getting settled in Palmyra, and she went out in the road and was run over by a truck. I rushed her to the Whitewater Veterinary Clinic and operated on her myself. She had suffered a fractured pelvis, and her skin had been torn away from her body over most of one side. Her recovery was quite uneventful, but she walked and ran with a decided limp and would tire very quickly when hunted. Some years later she developed an infection in her uterus called meteritis, and I put her to sleep so she would not suffer.

My second Dixie was a Britainy Spaniel who had been named before I got her. She was about two years old, and I could never figure out how her owner could give her away . He had purchased her as a puppy because of her bloodlines and wanted to breed her with his dog. For some unknown reason, she would not have anything to do with him. So he put an ad in the paper, and I rushed to his home in Lake Mills to claim her. I insisted on paying for her, as I told him any dog worth taking home was worth money. She proved to be an exceptional pet and a excellent hunting dog. I felt obliged to try and see if we could breed her after she had been separated from his dog for two years, but she obviously had not forgotten him and had not changed her mind. A year later we tried artificial insemination, but were again unsuccessful. A client with a registered male agreed to mate her for the pick of the litter, and we bred her. 61 days later she presented us with 16 tiny pups. Unfortunately we were only able to save two. The breeder took one male and I sold the other to a hunting buddy who had been very impressed with Dixie.

Chapter 45

My mother and dad were always going to travel when Dad retired from teaching, but the only trip Mother got was across the road to the cemetery, although she did come to Iowa once to visit me while I was in vet school. Olive's folks never did get to leave the state. I made up my mind that we were not going to wait until we were old and gray before we saw some of the world outside Wisconsin. I belong to the A.A.B.P (American Association of Bovine Practitioners), which held a yearly convention throughout the U.S., which usually lasted three or four days. For many years we attended, traveling to Atlanta, Columbus Ohio, Buffalo, San Francisco, San Antonio, Toronto, St. Louis, Baltimore, Kansas City and Seattle; reconnecting with friends and fellow veterinarians. Ten years after graduation, a group of my classmates went to Hawaii to visit a classmate who practiced there. Believe it or not, on the fourth day, we actually visited his vet clinic. We went back to Hawaii years later for a conference on skin conditions in small animals.

It was cost-prohibitive to travel with eight children until we had a motor home. The family went to Florida and Disney World a couple of times. We also went to New Orleans, Las Vegas, Maine and Cheyenne. It was on these trips that the kids developed a real sense of togetherness. Sixteen years ago, they complained they did not spend enough time to gather to get into a real disagreement, so CFV (Crawley Family Vacation) was born. Today, there are 34 members of Clan Crawley and we spend a week together every summer.

I arranged a trip to Alaska for ten of my clients and friends, some of whom had never been out of state. At the funeral of one of them, his wife told me that trip had been one of the best times of their lives. When I reached the age of 60, I decided if we were ever to go to Europe we had better get started. We traveled with Jerry and Dana to Ireland to trace all or family trees. The Crawleys were a bunch of drunken sheepherders (actually rebels and fighters), but the Curtins were scholars and statesman. We visited a small pub in Limerick, with red-haired Mary tending bar. When some off us ordered beer we learned that included lager, stout, or ale. When I asked for a Guiness, a fellow at the bar turned and said, "Good choice Lad. If the good Lord had anything better, he kept it for himself." We have also been to England and Scotland, but we enjoyed the Irish the most. We have been on three Caribbean cruises, which were fine, but I enjoyed our trips to the Dominican Republic more. I guess our worldwide trips are done as I don't want to be that far from home anymore.

Chapter 46

I sat motionless on the stump, straining my ears to hear the baying of the hounds as they drew ever nearer. Suddenly, a six-point buck came into view through the palmettos. I took aim with my shotgun, directly behind the front legs on the chest and fired once. He collapsed within five feet as the double ought buckshot blew out his heart and broke both front legs. They were not going to cut off my shirttail this morning!

To start at the beginning of this tale, I must go back to my purchasing a new shotgun at the base PX, and meeting the manager, Charles Bennett, a month or so earlier. When we started talking about hunting, he asked if I would like to go deer hunting on his two brothers' plantation in north Georgia when the season opened later that fall. On the first trip out I was placed on a stand in the swamp, and warned not to leave or they would cut out the seat of my hunting pants, and I figured these fellows meant business. They put Charles on another stand and left to release the dogs. About three hours later they came back to pick us up with the truck and proceeded to the place where Charles was standing. One of the brothers announced that he had heard a shot and asked, "Where is the deer?" Charles replied there was none, and they asked, "Where is the blood?" and again he shook his head. They announced that they found him guilty, and proceeded to cut off the shirttail of his fine hunting shirt and nail it to a tree.

So when they came to pick me up that morning and questioned, "Where is the deer?" I calmly pointed to the dead buck lying behind a tree. Then I made a big mistake when they asked if it was my first deer and I admitted it was. I was to be anointed in proper Georgia fashion, and they opened the body cavity, and retrieved a handful of blood which they smeared all over my face. It was a warm morning and it quickly dried. When we got back to the house for lunch the grandmother laughed and said, "Looks like Doctor got a deer."

We took it to the local processing plant to have it taken care of and a couple weeks later, when it dressed out, I took it back to the Base. I gave some venison to the fellows who worked for me, to some of the medical personnel at the hospital, and to our neighbors. When Olive tried to cook some of it, the smell nearly drove us out of the trailer, and no one ever asked for more. It was in Base cold storage and as far as I know it may be there yet.

Over the past 50 years, I have shot over 30 deer and none were ever as bad as the first one. I have never gotten a trophy head to hang on the wall, but it maybe just as well. My wife declares there will never be a deer head on our wall as long as we are married, and after 53 years I'm too tired to start looking.

Chapter 47

When I received a phone call last week that Joseph Von Rueden had been found dead in his swimming pool, my thoughts went back to the last time I had been called to his farm, in November of 1963. The Von Rueden farm had been in the family since the 1800's, and the Kau family had moved across the road in the 1940's. The Kaus had two sons and a daughter, while the Von Rueden family consisted of two daughters and a son. Maybe they married each other because it was a short trip for courting. Now all three were farmers and clients of mine.

Joseph and Marie had sold the farm to the Department of Natural Resources, and were going to move to California. It was the day of their farm auction to sell the cows, and one of them was having trouble delivering her calf. The barn was busy with people preparing the cows for sale. The animal I was interested in had four hind feet protruding from the vagina. I grasped the largest pair and attempted to pull them out, but the small pair which were above came also. I pushed them back into the uterus and attempted to pull the small pair, but, alas, the larger pair came also. After about 15 minutes, I decided I was going to have to remove the calf come what may. I put chains on the large pair of legs and attached them to the calf jack and removed it from a cow, and I discovered it was a fetal monster with six legs, with the four hind legs joined at the pelvis. I had never seen such a calf in all my years of practice.

Joseph had been breeding with American Breeding Service for many years and all of his cows were from those bulls. A new artificial inseminator had just started in our area, and had decided to put cards over each cow, with her name and production records to advertise ABS. He was up at the house finishing the cards when I decided to play a joke on him. His name was Tom Burke, and I asked him for a blank card to identify the new calf. He was all smiles and said he would be right down to the barn to look at it. When he saw it, his mouth dropped open and he pleaded to get rid of that animal before anyone saw it. I told him that I was going to charge 25 cents to view the six-legged calf, and I expected to make a lot of money telling people if they wanted such an animal, they had to breed ABS as they were the only company that produced such animals. Now he really became concerned that I would do such a thing, and he practically got on his hands and knees to beg me to destroy the monster. Everyone in the barn had a good laugh at Tom's expense.

Chapter 48

Over the years, I found making diagnoses as a large animal vet was like playing detective. First you studied the clues, examining and observing the animal, you listen to the farmer and ask questions, you narrow the possibilities, and make a deduction resulting in a diagnosis and possible cure. Such was the case with Bill Liesenfelder's sick cow. He had called early in the morning to report an animal having a serious respiratory problem and pleaded for me to get there as soon as possible. He lived about a half a mile from the highway, and his driveway was covered with snow over the top of my boots. There was no way I could drive back to the barn, so I grabbed two medicine cases and plowed ahead on foot.

When I reached the barn, Bill was anxiously awaiting my arrival; however the cow did not appear to be that sick. He apologized and said an hour earlier she could hardly breathe, with her mouth wide open, and tongue extended, gasping for air. I checked her temperature and listened to her lungs and could find nothing wrong. I asked him if he had treated her with anything and he shook his head no. I questioned when her symptoms had started, and he replied, "Shortly after she was fed." When I inquired if the feed was any different, he told me no, but he had started feeding from a different silo because the one on the north side of the barn was freezing. He acknowledged that the top part of the silo had been filled with corn with lots of weeds the previous fall. We had been told by some of our professors in vet school, we were very fortunate that animals did not have allergies, but I was very suspicious that under these circumstances I was dealing with a food allergy. I ask him to give her a forkful of silage, and with in minutes she was again gasping for air. I told him not to feed her any more from that silo until he got below the weeds.

Sometimes, however, you have to depend on serendipity to look smart. Bernard Jungles had moved to Wisconsin from northern

Indiana, where he had been a pig farmer. Now he was attempting to become a dairy farmer, and not too successfully. He had bought this farm and had spent several days with the owner milking the cows. However, on the day of the auction he got carried away and bought cows with bad udders. On top of that, he was a novice at bidding and the auctioneer had taken advantage of him, and raised the prices on the animals he bought. He once told me that the locals must have thought he was a real jackass. I had to agree and he asked, "Why did not someone tell me?" and I replied, "Who would you have listened to?"

Now he had a cow that was off feed and giving very little milk. I examined her thoroughly and could find no obvious reason for her condition. I started to check her teeth to see if that could be the cause, and when I put my hand in her mouth I could feel an electrical shock. The watering system had grounded out, and every time she started to drink she would get a shock, so she had quit drinking and was very dehydrated. I told him to get an electrician out there as soon as possible to find the cause. There was an old windmill in the barnyard with some electrical wires hanging down, and when the wind blew them against the steel they shorted out the water pipes.

Chapter 49

After reviewing that tale of the allergic cow, I was reminded of a couple more instances where I had to play detective. Carol Grant lived on a small farm on Island Road, just outside of town. She was an old maid, but a tough one, who shared her board (and perhaps her bed) with a fellow named Bob Block, who worked at the local feed mill. They milked about twelve animals and so if one of them died, it was a considerable loss. I found the dead cow lying across the gutter with her head pulled out of the stanchions, and it was obvious she had died in great pain. I performed a necropsy, but the only significant lesion I would find was a large bloody ulcer in the fourth stomach. I felt whatever substance had caused it had to be dissolved before it affected her. I checked the rest of the herd and there appeared nothing the worse for wear. Carol assured me there was no untoward matter in the feed. I searched the barnyard and found where they had been licking some barn lime. I was sure this was not the culprit, but it told me that they were lacking mineral and they would lick on anything they could find. There was a small shed at the edge of the barnyard with a partially broken window, and inside was a bench with a broken bag of fertilizer. I could see something had eaten about 2 tablespoons of it. This was the answer to my problem, and I told her she must repair the window and get some mineral for the rest of the herd.

Several years later, I was called to check some feedlot cattle that had been brought from the West for fattening outside of Mukwonago. Five businessmen thought they could make money fattening cattle under the name Bargo Beef. The people involved were to receive a percentage of the profit after the expenses were paid. Now there were three dead animals in a lot, and the profits were going down the drain unless I could find a reason. I did a post-mortem on each of them and again, the only significant lesion I could find was that same bloody ulcer in the fourth stomach. I was sure I was dealing with fertilizer poisoning again but alas, alack, I could find no evidence of fertilizer.

I questioned the feed mill that was supplying the feed, as to possible contamination of the feed during production or transportation, and was assured there could be nothing wrong. A couple of years later, one of my clients that worked at the mill told me, "Doc, you were a lot closer to the answer then you thought." The feed mill had attempted to keep their costs as low as possible, and so they used fertilizer grade urea rather than feed grade, and it contained contaminates.

Chapter 50

Over the years, I have been called many times to check animals that were struck and killed by lightning. Most farmers had insurance to cover such cases, but they needed a certificate from the vet and an appraisal. I found out early on not to appraise the animal at a higher value than they were insured for, as it only caused hard feelings between the farmer and the insurance company.

I had been called to the Gilson Brothers farm to check such an animal, and when I arrived they told me she was out in the pasture under a tree. It had rained the night before, and it gave all the appearances of a lightning strike, except for one small detail. In the wet grass you could see where they had dragged the cow with their tractor. When I got back up to the barn they said, "What do you think Doc?" I smiled and said, "Nice try fellows. Better luck next time. " They pleaded, "We have been paying for insurance for years and never collected". I assured them if they ever had a genuine claim, I would do my best to see them collect.

It was in late August -- we were suffering from a severe drought, and as it hadn't rained in nearly four weeks -- when I was called to Irvine Schulz farm to check a cow that he thought might have been struck by lightning. I had never been on this farm before and I could find no one around. I looked in the barn and all round the barnyard, even the fields next to the buildings, but no dead cow was to be seen. I was about to leave when he arrived from a cornfield where he had been cutting corn with a corn knife. The stalks were about to three feet in length, due to the drought. He was a rather tall old man, who walked with a stoop and dressed in ragged overalls. When I inquired where was the dead cow he said, "Behind the toolshed." There was a skeleton, and a litter of pigs running in and out of the chest cavity, and nothing much else. I explained him in order to have a lightning claim, we needed two things: lightning and a dead cow, and we didn't have either. I could not have determined if that cow had been hit by a

Mack truck, and we had had no lightning in nearly a month. He said there had been lightning in Beloit, but I explained that the cow had been in Palmyra. I was never called back to that farm again.

John E. Crawley, DVM

Chapter 51

The key to any successful livestock enterprise is like a three-legged milk stool, with one leg being genetics, the second nutrition, and lastly management. In most cases, the short leg is management, but this certainly was not the case with Elmer Marty. It was said he could get milk out of a chicken. He had developed one of the top-producing herds in the state of Wisconsin, and I was proud to be his veterinarian. Elmer had been the herdsman for the industrial school, which was a reform school for young boys, and when his father-in-law left his farm, Elmer took over.

You would find it hard to believe the extent of management practices he took with his cows. Sometimes in the winter, he would spend the entire day in the barn, caring for them. He kept the drinking cups scrupulously clean so that the water was always fresh. He swept the mangers and changed the hay three or four times a day so it was new. He brushed and curried each animal daily, and went over them with a vacuum cleaner at least once a week. In the summer they were allowed to walk, at their own pace, to and from the pasture, which was irrigated, and a fence rotated to give them fresh grass every week. The one pop innovation, which he claimed was the reason for his success, was that he had installed a water softener and the cows drank soft water in the barn. He could not explain to me what the difference was when the cows drank spring water six months a year in the pasture. The only thing he did that bothered me was he wanted his bull to be afraid of him, and it made it very difficult to treat the animal.

The Purina feed company was very proud to announce to everyone that he fed their ration to his herd. They appealed to him to try a new ration, called Dry and Freshening. Elmer said he did not want more production from his cows, but he would like them to be in better condition when they finished their lactations. He milked his cows for 365 days rather than the standard 305, as he felt most problems occurred after the animal has calved. He had been on the program for about six months when we began to have problems with fresh animals. They would retain their placentas after birth, go off feed, and develop mastitis. I knew Elmer was not very happy with me. I finally told him he had to change his feeding program, because the cattle were nutrition deficient. He did not question me, and immediately told Purina their ration was not doing the job and he was stopping it. I attended a feed meeting not long after that, and was cornered by the Purina representatives, who were not at all happy with me. I had always tried not to blame the health problems on the feed, but I was sure in this case I was correct. They brought their nutritional experts and top brass to visit the farm, and their conclusion was their ration was fine, but he had an exceptional herd, so he had to feed twice their recommendations. He just laughed, and said that would cost him double and he would stay with his original decision.

Elmer had one son, Gordon, who helped on the farm. When Elmer decided to quit milking, Gordon knew he was not ready to devote the time and effort to the cows that his dad had. If they were to remain friends, he must choose a different path, so the cattle were sold at auction. A couple of them went to another client, who could not duplicate their milk records. He accused Martys of falsifying them, but I assured him they were accurate and true.

Chapter 52

Irving R. Young was an enigma. On the one hand he was a philanthropic millionaire and an engineering genius, but on the other hand he was an eccentric, self-centered despot. He owned two factories: a printing plant in Neenah and a engineering plant in Palmyra, called Snow Valley Engineering. He had built hospitals for lepers in Africa, a sawmill for their employment, and donated a guerrilla to the Lincoln Park Zoo in the Chicago. I'm sure there were many other good things he had done that I don't know.

I first met him through a girlfriend who lived near his countryside home, which was filled with trophies from Africa. About four years late, I received a modern wrought iron table lamp has a wedding present that he brought to my parents' home. It set the stage for decorating our first home in Ames, Iowa. I did not see or hear from him again until I was setting up practice. He called to tell me that he would like to build a small animal hospital and clinic for us in Palmyra. I had seen and heard what happened to people who he had helped, where he would dictate how they ran their business, and I wanted none of that. I had witnessed how he treated his workers like dirt. I once met a man who told me that he had worked for Mr. Young, and when I inquired for how long, he said he almost made it until noon. I told Irv that I wanted to wait to see if I liked the town and it liked me. He owned two farms and a herd of Black Angus cattle and wanted me to be the herdsmen for them. I said I would be glad to do the vet work, but I had not gone to college for eight years to be a herdsman.

He had grandiose plans and ideas, which didn't always work out as well as he hoped. He built a large, self-feeding barn in which the chopped hay was supposed to keep gradually sliding down to the mangers for the cattle. Unfortunately, it didn't work that way. One day I was called to examine four cows that had suffocated when the hay had come loose and buried them. Another one of his ill-fated schemes was to build a water skiing facility near his home. He dug a large pond, put an island in middle, and placed a truck with a boom over the water that pulled a skier while the boom went around in circles. He was going to build a milking parlor where the cows were on a merry go round and the milker stayed in one place. He became very upset with me when I tried to explain the fallacy of his idea. He did build some equipment to solve problems he encountered. When he built the factory in Palmyra using cement blocks, he thought they were too expensive at 27 cents apiece, so he decided to make his own. It was the middle of winter, and the sand and gravel were both frozen, so he manufactured a heating and drying machine to thaw them so he could make cement. Years later, we had a very wet year and the corn did not ripen, so he adapted the equipment to dry his corn, and it worked well. My brother brought two agricultural engineers from the University to see it. They were impressed, and wanted to know when he was going into production. He told them his corn was dry, and he would sell them the plans for $100,000 dollars.

On top of a hill behind the plant, he built a lodge that housed a rope ski tow that was going to be a great attraction for skiers throughout the area. Unfortunately, it never caught on and stands empty to this day. He also constructed about ten sculptures made of scrap iron that remain in the fields and along the hillside. He once told me that he was going to build a church on top of a large hill, with the roof shaped like a pair of praying hands. When I remarked that it sounded like the Unitarian church in Madison, designed by Frank Lloyd Wright, he scoffed and said, "Wright couldn't design a barn." His most successful venture was designing and building printing presses, which he never sold. He only leased to various companies, so the plant in Palmyra continues to operate, to maintain and repair those machines. For many of them, there were no blueprints and the plans were only in his head.

Our relationship ended when I sent him a bill for doing post-mortems on four dead cows. The sides of a large grain bin had broken open and large amounts of dry soybeans had spilled out onto the ground, and the cattle had gorged themselves on the beans. When they drank water, the beans swelled and they died of bloat. I explained the cause

John E. Crawley, DVM

of death, but he insisted I should post them, so I did. I submitted tissue samples to the state lab to make sure there had been no disease. He was sure that I had never charged him for other posts I had done, but I explained I had done them for my benefit, to check my diagnosis. This time he asked for a service, and I provided it.

He died in 1976 at the age of 79, and he was buried in an old cemetery near his home. He had collected so much stuff in the plant it took three days to sell it all. There were nearly 40 old bakery trucks that he had purchased to send to Africa, to be used as ambulances, and he had already sent some. There were over 100 guns of all shapes and sizes, along with 50 small refrigerators and countless pieces of equipment.

His widow established the Irving L. Young foundation, which has provided funds for the track and field at the high school and the Irving L. Young Community Center in Palmyra. In Whitewater, it funded the Irving L. Young Memorial Library and the Irving L. Young Center for the Performing Arts on the campus of UW Whitewater, so his name will remain prominent for years and years to come.

Chapter 53

In the spring of 1967, a young farm boy from Carroll, Iowa graduated from Iowa State College of Veterinary Medicine, and less than a month later was in Sullivan, Wisconsin, applying for a job with Tri-County Veterinary Service, Incorporated. Dan Stark appeared to be a good fit for our practice. However, it was equally important that his wife, Jennifer, could adapt to living in a small town. After our experience with Betty Mirtz, we did not want to find ourselves in the same boat again. So after a meal, together with all the wives, we agreed to offer him a contract.

That proved to be one of the best decisions we were ever to make. The corporation had purchased the home and office of a retired doctor in Sullivan, and it was agreed that they would move into it as soon as possible, and begin to work with Dr. Phelps. They began their family soon after, and ended up with four fine boys. A few years later, we invited him to become one of the partners in the corporation, and the proper papers were drawn up and signed by all. Dan was rather easy-going and not too excitable. He is a good veterinarian, but his greatest attribute to me was his ability to put up with Dr. Phelp's eccentricities. He never complained, although privately we would chuckle about them. He was well accepted by the farmers and small animal clients, and was a genuine asset to the business.

As their family grew, they outgrew the old doctor's house, so they built a new home outside of town, where the boys had room to grow and play. The practice work schedule was set up so each one of us had one weekend a month off. I was the swingman, covering the Mukwonago practice along with the Palmyra area one weekend, and working the Sullivan / Palmyra practice the other two. I was the only one in the practice who was acquainted with all of the clients.

When Dr. Phelps developed complications of hepatitis after a blood transfusion, and had to retire, Dan took over the Sullivan practice

John E. Crawley, DVM

alone until he could hire another vet. He was very good to the Phelps family during John's illness and after his death. I still admire and respect him as a veterinarian, businessman, husband, father and friend.

Chapter 54

Wyatt Earp rode into town the summer of 1958 in a bright red Studebaker Hawk, vowing to restore law and order to the village of Palmyra as the new police chief. His real name was Leroy Dutton. He had worked at American Motors in Kenosha, and he moved to a home across the street from where we were living. He was a tall, well built man in his early 40's. He wore a brimmed hat, much like those worn by the state highway patrol, and on his leg was strapped a quick draw holster containing a long barrel 45 caliber revolver; hence the name, "Wyatt Earp." One day he was mowing the lawn in his usual garb when my oldest son, who was 4 years old at the time, called over and asked, "Mister, if you are going to play cowboy can I play with you?"

There soon developed an animosity between him and the teenagers of the town, who were constantly harassing him. On one occasion they put a half a pound of sugar in his gas tank while he parked downtown, and of course it damaged the motor. He would frequent the taverns in town and the neighboring villages, and one time, when he was feeling no pain in an Eagle saloon someone stole his gun from it's holster.

One Sunday afternoon he was attending a gathering that the Fred Kellen farm, and the boys, teasing him about his marksmanship, challenged him to hit a 50-cent piece in the air. Lo, miracle of miracles, he hit one and the coin when flying into a field. He said he would pay $10 for that coin, and the Kellen boys, being no fools, put a 50-cent piece in a vise, drilled a hole through it, and collected the $10. For a long time he carried it in his pocket to show, until finally the true story came back to him.

My only direct contact occurred one evening in the drugstore, when he asked me where he could get a mean Doberman to put in his car to guard a prisoner, and if he made a bad move the dog would chew him up. I solemnly declared I did not know where he would find such a dog. There was a young high-school girl working behind the counter

John E. Crawley, DVM

and she added, "I don't know where you could find such a prisoner." He quickly turned on his heel and left the store without another word.

His entire career as police chief came to an in ignominious end on Halloween, 1960. The previous year the boys had decorated the downtown in the usual manner, with bundles of cornstalks, signs, and a vast array of used farm machinery. He had vowed that would never happen again, so when the Halloween came, on Friday night, he enlisted the help of the Jefferson County deputies. They parked downtown and followed teenagers in their cars until the early morning, and the deputies told him they had better things to do.
On Saturday night he deputized to the entire village board, and they spent the evening following the kids until early morning, and they told them they were not going to waste another evening watching kids. Sunday night the kids stuck with of vengeance. While he would be chasing one group, another would pile cornstalks and garbage on the street, and when he would go after them, another group would bring the farm machinery downtown. The next day he went to George Murn, the implement dealer, and wanted him to swear out a warrant for taking the machinery, but George told him they had done no harm, these kid's fathers were customers, and he would not press charges against them.

The boys had borrowed an International pickup truck that belonged to a Art Schmidt, a local garage owner, to haul the cornstalks and signs around town, and Wyatt wanted him to press charges for stealing his truck. Art told him if George would, he might consider it, but otherwise no dice. When he threatened to give him a ticket for leaving the keys in the truck parked on the street, Art blew up and told him it had been left on his property. "Someone else had borrowed the truck on Saturday and left the keys in the ignition, and now get the hell out of my garage before I get mad. "

When the municipal court met the next week, he presented the names of fifteen young teenagers to be charged. When questioned by Judge Walter Shepard, he had to admit that he had not actually seeing any of them doing mischief, but he insisted they must be guilty. The judge insisted that unless he actually saw them, they could not be charged. At this point, Wyatt stated he would resign if they were not prosecuted, and Walter said, "Goodbye and good luck." Wyatt went home and removed the red light from his car that evening, and returned to Kenosha shortly after.

He was replaced by a real police officer from Madison by the name of Lester Shore, who made a great attempt to restore respect for the department, especially with the young people. The next Halloween eve, he parked downtown and watched the kids decorate the area as usual, but did nothing to stop them. The next morning, and he went to the high school and congratulated them on a fine job. Then he told them it was time to clean up. That was 45 years ago, and there has never been any vandalism on Halloween since.

Chapter 55

Pat and Mia Blair believed that the road to financial success ran through a pigpen -- not any pen, but one that contained those cute little Vietnamese potbellied pigs. And so they made their first mistake; they went to Minnesota and purchased three piglets. All sports fans are aware that you get hogs in Arkansas; in Minnesota you get gophers.

They weren't aware that they needed Interstate Health papers, and so the piglets were in quarantine until they could be blood-tested by the state lab. Normally, you bleed hogs with a needle in the heart, but there is a small danger of mortality in this process. They had paid $1,400 for the boar (male) and $1,200 apiece for the two sows (female) and I was not going to take a chance on losing one of them. I bled them from their ear veins. These piglets were six months old and weighed about five pounds apiece, so you can imagine how small the veins were.

The next the next time I went to the farm to check on them, they showed me where they were kept. It was a large barn, and it had three large pens with walls about three feet high. They had spread leaves and grass in each pen to a depth of about ten inches. I told them the sows would never be able to feed the piglets with that much bedding. They also had to make a better exit for them -- they were crawling under the walls to go outside and they would injure their backs, which could paralyze them. A pig has a very weak back and I have seen large pigs killed by a shovelful of corn.

The next visit was a maternity call; I was to check the mothers and their babies. The first pen contained a mother and two babies, but the second pen held a mother only. They insisted there were three babies there, but alas there were not. When they asked me what had happened, I told them they didn't want to know. They insisted, and when I told them the mother had eaten the young they were greatly dismayed.

When the two survivors were three months old they decided to take them to Texas for a huge Vietnamese potbellied pig sale. Alas, again they forgot they needed health papers to take them across state lines, and so at the last moment I had to bleed these two. They hand-carried them in the airline, but the sale was less than a success, and they didn't even make enough money to pay the airfare.

At this point, they decided they were not cut out to be pig farmers, so they sent the three remaining pigs to be slaughtered and to be and made into Italian sausage. Unfortunately, they could not bear to eat any of it because it reminded them of the three little pigs. Eventually, I received some of the Italian sausage.

Now about this time, I had a daughter getting married on the island of St. Croix, and at the wedding dinner, we drank and celebrated. We were nearly done when the waitress approached our table with a bottle of Dom Perignon champagne, which sells for over a hundred dollars a bottle. I insisted that we save it for a celebration when we got home, and so at Easter when all the family was here we shared it. What do you serve with a hundred-dollar bottle of champagne? How about $4,000 worth of Italian sausage?

John E. Crawley, DVM

Section Four: Tails of Another Cow Doc
(Jerry's Story)

Hi John and Arla,
Dana and I finished your book, and now Jack and Olive are reading it.
I am at Castle Rock Lake with them this weekend. We fished for five
hours this morning, and only caught two fish.

I enjoyed your book very much. Ours were very similar lives. Your
Aunt Helen was a mean old cripple, and every time I would get in
range she hit me with her cane. Russ Chapman and I got under her
bed once, and started to bounce her around with our feet until we
bounced her right out of bed on to the floor. Mother was directing
play practice at the high school, so I had to run and get her and tell her
what we had done.

I can't remember an age when I didn't have to help in the garden, feed
the chickens, or pick up eggs. We always raised 150 chicks and sold
the roosters as springers and sold eggs. First Jack and then I would
sell vegetables around the village in our little wagons. Jack had a
paper route and I took it over when I was 10. One summer I pedaled
the Sentinel in the morning, the Journal in the afternoon and the
Freeman at night. I had the Freeman route until we moved to the farm
in 1950. We always had several garden spots, with lots of
strawberries and raspberries to pick and sell, and also a large pickle
patch. From the time I was 12 to 17, I also had pickles of my own to
pick. I also mowed three cemeteries. There was never a doubt that we
were going to college, and all we ever heard was put any money we
got into the bank for school.

Dad used to beat us, especially Jack quite often, but he never hit
mother. We used to take a bath and get a change of clothes once per
week. Never had shoes in the summer nor wore a shirt. Was always
"encouraged" to get A's in school, and I was told that if I didn't get
straight A's in high school, I could not go out for sports. I lettered in

baseball as a freshman and in basketball and football as a junior and senior. I was selected as the outstanding high school athlete in my senior year. I was in the band and choir and all the class plays. I was in FFA and became a "state farmer". I also won the speech contests two years and was valedictorian of my class. I got a scholarship to University of Wisconsin, and like you, I kept track of every penny I spent. My first year cost $1,000, and I stayed in Madison with one of my dad's aunts, and walked a mile along the railroad tracks to agricultural school.

I took Agricultural Education as a major, and when mom died I was a junior. I came home on Friday, October 9th, and mom told me she wanted me to quit school and take over the farm, as she was going to die that night. She seemed perfectly fine to me and I said, "What are you talking about?" She had a "black out" over three hours long that day. She said she had been to heaven and saw God. That there was a bright light that she followed and everything was bright, beautiful and peaceful, and that now she was not afraid to die. They had told her that she would die that night. I helped Dad finished the milking, and he went into the basement and stayed there crying all night. Mom had a heart attack about 1:00 a.m. Saturday. They didn't have a family doctor so I called all over trying to get her into a hospital. I finally got a doctor in Elkhorn to admit her. I had called Jack in Ames to come home. He drove all night and got home just as they called from hospital to say she died.

Dad never went to the barn from then until some time of about mid December. He would lie on her grave in the cemetery and cry all the time. Then one Sunday morning, I came in from the barn with a little manure on my shoe. He pointed that out to me, and said that I had killed mother. He punched me in the face and knocked me down twice, and said he was going to kill me. I grabbed my car keys and took off for Ames and Jack. I stopped at my Uncle George's, and told them to watch out for my dad and the cows, and that I was going to Iowa to see Jack. We went to see a psychologist, and he said Dad sounded like a manic-depressive and that he would probably kill me and that we should get him into treatment as soon as possible. We had tried to get him to see a doctor, but he wouldn't, so Jack said, "I

John E. Crawley, DVM

will have to commit him when I come home at Christmas", and that's what he did. All of our aunts and uncles except one turned on us. I lived by myself and took care of the farm until the end of March. I never felt Mendota did anything to help my dad, but the shock of the cops coming and hauling him out of the bed cured him. He never forgave Jack, and never liked me much either.

The next spring, an old neighbor who had no relatives said that if I would take over his farm and take care of him and his wife, he would give me all his land and livestock. So I said, "Well, let me see how goes milking at two places." It went okay. One day I started out of our place with the tractor and plow, and Dad came running out and asked me what I thought I was doing. I said I was going to Bill's to plow and he said, "No you are not. That is my machinery, and it is not leaving this farm." It was then I knew I had to go back to school. I had not made any money farming our place, so I went looking for a job and got one at Hein Warner at $1.70 an hour.

I would get up at 4:00 a.m., do chores and milking, and leave for work at 6:00 a.m., picking up four other guys, and get home about 4:30 to do chores and milking again. Dad did let the cows out for water and clean the barn while I was at work. Then in late July, I told him one Sunday that we were playing for first place with the baseball team, and that if we won I wasn't coming home to milk that night. I had never had a day off since my mother died. Well you guessed it; when I got home at 9:00 p.m., the cows were not milked. I did that, and then came into the house and told him I was done milking cows, and if he didn't do it tomorrow it wasn't going to get done. He got up, milked the cows, then came into the house and told me to get out. I did, and that fall I went back to school. He sold the herd in the middle of August, and I went home to get them prepared for sale. I believe by then, third of them belonged to me. I had bought my first purebred Heifer calf when I was 10. Anyway, I got about $5,000, so with what I saved from working (later, I got a piecework job and made $3 an hour) and with that, I had enough to pay for the rest of Madison. I made the decision to try to get in to vet school. I was turned down my first try, but in the second attempt I got accepted at Iowa State, Cornell, Penn State's and Minnesota.

Dana and I got married August 29th 1959, and Jane came July 25th 1960, Gerrieann March 7, 1962, John March 30, 1963, Kenneth April 19, 1965 and Tim March 30, 1969. Like you, I was working most of the time and she raised the kids. I tried to get to most of their activities, but missed way too many. Chris came as a real surprise in January of 1979.

Like you, I had a lot of illness. Besides all of the regular childhood diseases, I had scarlet fever when I was five and nearly died. I was delirious most of the time. I had a tonsillectomy later, and an appendectomy six days before going into the Army. I also had trouble with the Army and joined the Reserves in 1955 to escape the draft. When I went back to school, I took the advanced ROT. Then I got deferred for vet school, but I had orders to report in May 1962, right after graduation. But in the meantime, I applied for and received a commission in the vet Corps. Thanks to a sergeant in Chicago, things got straightened out and I went to Fort Sam Houston in Texas on January 1st 1963. After basic training there, I was assigned to do research at the Germ Warfare Center in Frederick Maryland. When we got there, Dana was very pregnant with John, and no base housing was available. They put us in temporary bachelor officers' quarters and all our stuff was in storage. Luckily, a lot of the 1961 Iowa State graduates were stationed there, and they fixed us up with baby beds, cooking utensils, etc. I became violently ill with severe abdominal pain. They sent me to Walter Reed twice but they could never make a diagnosis. Dana finally had John and we'd found a place to rent just off the base and I got well. After we got to Mukwonago for a few years, I was in the hospital for two weeks with some sort of pneumonia. Later I got encephalitis, and then I had a heart attack. I broke a few ribs in 1978, and started to become weak and cold all of the time. Finally in March 1988, I had a grand mall seizure while at the hospital taking a stress test. That week in the hospital, they found the tumor and you know the rest.

John E. Crawley, DVM

Jack and I were always very small. He was 5 ft. 2 in. when he graduated from high school, and I was five-foot 6 in. and weighed 120 pounds. He grew 6 inches in college, and I grew 4 inches, but I never weighed over 150 lbs. until after my first brain surgery.

I got a research fellowship for two years from the Mark Morris foundation. This paid me $2,400 a year, and Dana worked for a dentist for a total of about 1 1/2 years, so we never had to borrow money for school, but we were dead broke when I graduated. I was able to take graduate credits along with vet credits, and went to school year-round for three summer schools. I graduated top in my class, and got my MS in Veterinary Physiology after I wrote my thesis. They had me teach Vet Pharmacology, and we stayed at Iowa State until I had my appendectomy in December. Jack and Dad came to pick us up and take us back to Palmyra, where Dana and the kids stayed while I was in Texas.

I had reunited with my Dad in the spring of my junior year at Madison. He was taken to the hospital, and the lady I had lived with called and told me I had better go to visit him, and I did it do that. I had ROTC summer camp for six weeks, and no job. He paid me $150 to shingle the barn and toolshed. I hate high places, but somehow I managed to get it done.

Dana thinks you must be a wonderful man: bright, generous and industrious. I told her that describes me too. Religious -- on that part, I'm left out. I'm a Christian, but I don't really believe in the church.

Good luck to you both.

As ever,
Jerry

Afterword

John Earl "Jack" "Doc" Crawley died on Wednesday, Aug. 25, 2010, at Fort Memorial Hospital of pulmonary fibrosis. He died as he lived - surrounded by love.

Doc was born on Nov. 5, 1929, to Eleanor (Wilton) and Earl H. Crawley in Ashland. He graduated from East Troy High School and went on to earn a bachelor's degree from the University of Wisconsin in Madison. He earned his Doctorate of Veterinary Medicine from Iowa State University.

Doc was a member of the ROTC at Iowa State University, and served in the U.S. Air Force in Savannah, Ga., and for many years in the Air Force Reserve. He retired with the rank of Major.

Upon completion of his Air Force active duty, Doc moved to Palmyra to begin his veterinary practice, which spanned over 50 years. His "COW DOC" license plates were a familiar and welcome site to farmers in three counties, and he cared for innumerable family pets from the clinic behind his house.

Doc loved Palmyra, and he put his heart and soul into making the community a better place to live and raise a family. He was a member of the Palmyra-Eagle School Board for nine years, including serving as president. He was an active member of Kiwanis for over 40 years, and loved his involvement in providing Christmas baskets for families, and with their sponsored youth programs. He was a leader in working to help young people avoid alcohol and other drug abuse, and he helped establish the first AODA program at Palmyra-Eagle High School. He was a faithful member of St. Mary's Catholic Church, and served on the Parish Council on multiple occasions.

Doc loved his family, and anyone who ever spoke to him was well aware of that. He is survived by his wife of nearly 57 years, Olive; and his children, Kevin (fiance Yvonne Bitticks-Maruniak), Kathleen (Timothy Dybevik), Ellen (Mark Thorn), Sara (Steve Poser), Colleen

John E. Crawley, DVM

(Doug Schell), Dennis (Jane Pacheco), Ann (Jeff Gerner) and Patrick (Kerry Odell). He further is survived by 16 adoring grandchildren, Andrew, Robin and Joseph Dybevik, Elizabeth, Kathleen and Hannah Thorn, Samuel and Gabriel Poser, Lauren and Patrick Schell, Gavin and Kiera Crawley, Christian and Alexander Gerner, and Liam and Emmett Crawley.

He is further survived by his brother, Gerald Crawley, who also was his partner in veterinary medicine and friend for his entire life; and by his brothers-in-law, Patrick and Larry Curtin; and sisters-in-law, Mary Curtin, Dana Crawley and Carol Anchor. He was preceded in death by his parents; his daughter-in-law, Diana Paulina; and many brothers and sisters-in-law.

Doc loved to fish - in addition to special trips with his brother Jerry and fishing buddies, he enjoyed many hours of fishing at Castle Rock and Pettenwell lakes with very special family and friends.

Doc loved to play cards, and was a long-time member of the Dirty Old Men's Poker and Spannferkel Society. The group provided more than good company and cards. They also raised funds for many causes in the Palmyra-Eagle School District, including athletic field lights and band uniforms.

Doc loved his trombone music. He was a proud member of the University of Wisconsin Marching Band, and in his later years a very active member of the Palmyra Community Band. He was an inveterate storyteller, and he had a joke for every occasion.

Doc said he had three goals in life: to be a veterinarian, to marry a beautiful woman and to raise a good family. He lived a long and happy life, and endured his more recent health challenges with courage and grace in anticipation of his journey to heaven.

Katie Crawley
August, 2010

John E. Crawley, DVM